Advance Praise for *PR Therapy*

"I have been in the public relations business for over 50 years. This is the best book I have seen. It covers every facet of the business that is necessary in order to be successful. Further, the way Robin Blakely has sectioned the book is excellent and presents a logical sequence of learning steps."

—**Howard Boasberg**, executive director of the Advertising Icon Museum

"Clear, therapeutic, and action oriented! *PR Therapy* provides excellent advice and how-to from a proven expert in her field."

—**Alan Flory**, President and CEO of ReDiscover

"*PR Therapy* is a precise, concise, and easy-to-understand prescription for achieving success. With clarity and in plain talk, Robin Blakely has created an ingenious, yet simple plan to guide us through the PR maze. Step-by-step, she outlines realistic methods that produce proven results. Robin's handbook for personal PR know-how is a must read for anyone who wants to take their career from so-so to sensational."

—**Hazel Dixon-Cooper**, author of the internationally best-selling *Rotten Day* book series, and *Cosmopolitan Magazine*'s "Bedside Astrologer"

"Finally! PR help that's personal, practical, and practically magic."

—**Rebecca Forster**, *USA Today* bestselling novelist and screenwriter

"Knowing that the quality of your life or business depends on the quality of the questions you ask yourself, Robin Blakely certainly offers great questions (and then some) to get anyone moving towards and reaching the business life of their dreams."

—**Karen Rauch Carter**, author of the national bestseller *Move Your Stuff, Change Your Life*

"Robin Blakely, a public relations pro, has written a brilliant handbook. It's not about tooting your own horn, but about marketing a message. *PR Therapy* banishes fear and insecurity."

—**Suzette Martinez Standring**, syndicated columnist and author of *The Art of Column Writing*

"Ever-entertaining longtime PR guru Robin Blakely puts the fun in marketing fundamentals."

—**Jamie Novak**, author of the #1 bestseller *1,000 Best Organizing Secrets*

"Highly recommended. Robin Blakey's innovative approach to planning and implementing promotional strategies is on the mark! *PR Therapy* has already changed my thinking about how to find and reach my audience."

—**Sandra Kitt**, recipient of two Lifetime Achievement Awards from RWA, and national bestselling author of *For All We Know*

"Robin Blakely's passion is helping the rest of us ignite ours to achieve the things we dream. *PR Therapy* is more than just a handbook for promoting your message—it's all the encouragement, insight, and support that Robin offers her clients each and every day. I know...I'm lucky enough to be one."

—**Marybeth Hicks**, columnist for *The Washington Times* and author of *Bringing Up Geeks*

"Robin Blakely covers it all....By the end of *PR Therapy* you have the tools and knowledge to promote yourself, feel good about rising to the top of your game, and stay true to your vision—with the steadfast belief that you absolutely can share your product with the world."

—**Sylvia Mendoza**, author of *The Book of Latina Women: 150 Vidas of Passion, Strength and Success*

"Robin Blakely is the real deal—an energetic, revolutionary PR guru—who finally wrote it all down. *PR Therapy* gives you a step-by-step process and tons of great tips. If you or your business needs a shot in the arm but are not quite sure where to begin, start with this book!"

—**Stacey Wolf**, author of *Psychic Living* and *Never Throw Rice at a Pisces*

PR THERAPY

IGNITE YOUR PASSION FOR PROMOTING YOUR
PRODUCTS, SERVICES, AND EVEN YOURSELF!

Robin Blakely

Fresno, CA

Copyright © 2009 by Robin Blakely. All rights reserved.

Published by Quill Driver Books
an imprint of Linden Publishing
2006 S. Mary, Fresno, California 93721
559-233-6633 / 800-345-4447
QuillDriverBooks.com

Quill Driver Books and Colophon are trademarks of
Linden Publishing, Inc.

Quill Driver Books project cadre:
Doris Hall, Dave Marion,
Stephen Blake Mettee, Kent Sorsky, Maura Zimmer

ISBN: 978-1-884956-97-3 (1-884956-97-1)

135798642
Printed in the United States of America on acid free paper.

Library of Congress Cataloging-in-Publication Data

Blakely, Robin.
  PR therapy : ignite your passion for promoting your products, services,
and even yourself! / Robin Blakely.
      p. cm.
  Includes index.
  ISBN-13: 978-1-884956-97-3 (pbk. : alk. paper)
  ISBN-10: 1-884956-97-1 (pbk. : alk. paper)
  1. Public relations. 2. Publicity. I. Title.
  HD59.B563 2009
  659.2--dc22
                              2008055808

For my husband Mark Stroginis,
whose first conversation with me
included the words that literally captured my heart:
"I Can Do Anything"…and who then, better still,
actually lived up to his promise.

CONTENTS

FOREWORD

I was in the back of a limousine on the verge of tears. I was supposed to be heading to a book signing in Connecticut, about an hour and fifteen minutes away. Only, the limo driver didn't know where to go.

"Where are you headed?" he asked, as though he were driving a taxi and I'd just hailed him from a city sidewalk. Except he was driving a limo hired by the department store that had bought a few hundred copies of my first book to give away at several customer appreciation events.

"Aren't *you* supposed to know that?" I asked him, exasperated.

It had been a very long month. First, the original publisher for my book pulled out just two weeks before the publication date, even though *Parenting* magazine had already plugged it and *Parents* was about to excerpt it. After landing another small publisher, my book was published, but, as I soon discovered, it was only available in a few bookstores and online. Then I drove three hours to a book signing only to discover that—whoopsies!—the store manager had forgotten to promote it. And now the limo driver didn't know where we were going.

So, I called Robin.

Robin Blakely had signed on as my publicist just a few months before my first book was to be published, and she was already proving to be more than a tireless promoter of my writing. She was my PR therapist.

"The limo driver doesn't know how to get there!" I sobbed into the phone.

"Okaaaaay," Robin soothed. "Let's see how we can fix it." And then she did. In the years to come, she'd fix many more PR situations for me, not all of them requiring Kleenex.

Since then, Robin has not only helped me promote my books and my website, she's helped me build a brand. Nowadays, it's essential to carefully and strategically add planks to your platform—the very foundation of your following, the basis of what makes you and your work marketable.

Thanks in no small part to Robin, I went from a newbie author of a book with distribution problems, lost in a limo and flying by the seat of my pants, to the owner of a successful website, spokesperson for major corporations, web consultant, blogger for top media outlets, media source, and author of several books, including a three-book series branded to my website, MommaSaid.net. But it didn't happen overnight, and it wasn't always easy. Yet with Robin's help, I was able to keep an eye on the bigger picture—the one with a view of next month, next quarter, next year and beyond—while working diligently on what absolutely had to be done today. And I did it all pretty darn fast.

Robin taught me to always think through exactly how our publicity efforts, no matter how small, could bring me something bigger down the road. If I appeared on a radio show in Chicago, for example, she'd ask if there were any PR firms, publishers, or corporations who should know about it, affording me even more opportunities. Now, when I get booked on a national TV show, she thinks through who we should tell in case there's someone who might hire me to write something or someone who needs a spokesperson. She taught me to look beyond the adrenaline-pumping excitement of the PR "get" in the short run and to think of it as another piece of my platform.

Most of all, Robin taught me to consider all of my PR efforts in the context of what's truly important to me. For instance, I knew that I didn't want to travel a lot while my kids were little, so we put speaking engagements on the back burner. And I know that the thing I like the most about my career is the opportunity to write, so we always place writing jobs at the top of my annual PR plan.

Finally, Robin is simply one of the most honest, caring, smart, creative, and kind people I've ever worked with, and I'm fortunate to know her. Her book is a collection of classic "Robinisms" put on paper, a big taste of what it's like to get to work with a brilliant mind that's filled with compassion, wit, and humor. And even if you never get to call her from the back of a limo, sobbing, you will learn a great deal from her in the pages of this book. I know I sure have.

—Jen Singer, creator of MommaSaid.net and author of the *Stop Second Guessing Yourself* parenting series

PHASE I

Your Big Couch Trip

One Saturday night about nine years ago I got a phone call out of the blue from a noted psychologist who needed a little PR therapy. This woman had crossed paths earlier that day with one of my clients at a business function. The two women hit it off, and somehow my work was discussed. The call still remains firmly etched in my brain.

The symptoms were classic. The psychologist was freaking out because her career had wandered up the road-less-traveled into an ugly, unknown territory. Then, in the frenzy of being lost, she began to deeply question her professional identity—she'd lost sight of where she was going, how she had ever imagined she'd get there, and why on God's green earth she had chosen this particular direction in the first place.

She described her personal turmoil using imagery universal to anyone who has ever been exhausted by the pursuit of a dream: "I'm burning out. I can feel it. I'm worn out from running in endless circles, falling repeatedly in bottomless quicksand, banging my head against the proverbial brick wall, and being told 'no' by everyone I encounter."

She simply didn't know whether to give in or give up. She cared way too much to quit, but she knew in her gut that she couldn't keep up the current pace forever. "I'm at the end of my rope…and I only need three things from you."

So there I stood, barefoot, on my back patio, already chin deep in her desperation and despair.

I assessed the situation. Here was a woman with enough burning intensity over the phone to start a fire, she had accomplishments longer than I was tall, and she was formally trained in the field of psychology at an Ivy League school. There was only one thing to do. I followed my heart and said, "You say you're at the end of your rope, and you only need three things from me. What are the three things?"

"I want you to tell me who I am, what I'm doing, and how to make it work."

It seems funny now, but in that instant this insightful stranger summed up the very thing I could do. For her, and many clients, a simple couch trip changes everything.

Now it's your turn.

PR Breakthroughs—
Not Personal Breakdowns

"I just opened my own business...."
"I just designed my first line of handbags...."
"I just got my garage band out of the garage and onto a real stage...."

For one magic moment you recognize that you've got what it takes to get your phone to ring off the hook, snag a spot on Oprah, and maybe earn even more money than Donald Trump.

But, then, it happens.

You realize with astounding clarity that your time to arrive *has* actually arrived. Suddenly, a flood of adrenaline causes your blood pressure to spike to near-stroke level. Your need for real publicity is now, *this instant*. Everything you've worked for appears to be at stake; the opportunity to win or lose everything rests squarely on your ability to promote yourself, your services, or your products.

The clock is ticking for you to perform. You're scared, you don't know where to start, and instead of kicking into promotional high gear, you're muttering like a madman: "Whatta I do....Whatta I do....Whatta I do?"

Okay—so what do you do?

First, slow down. Take a deep breath. Get a grip. You aren't doomed, you don't suck, and the light at the end of the tunnel isn't an oncoming train—it's your bright future. It's time to feel good about your ability to get the publicity you need. It's time for you to pull yourself up by your PR bootstraps and make things happen.

Question One: *"Can I Find a Way to Get Started?"*

Yes, you can. You have to start where you are and with what you've got. But, first, you need to know that you do actually have a real chance to succeed.

You do.

It's normal to have some doubts about the PR process. The truth is you're not alone: Most people don't know how to publicize who they are or to promote what they do. With so many media choices—cable TV, major network TV, radio, magazines, newspapers, newsletters, as well as Twitter, blogs, and the entire Internet—it's no wonder that the task of where to start and where to go may, at first, seem overwhelming.

The choices appear endless—and luckily they are—because choices are actually opportunities, and there are literally hundreds waiting for you. You don't have to be a PR expert to succeed. It's possible for you to do what it takes and to do it really well. Part of what got you this far has worked, and it can keep working.

Here's why: You've been steadily building a track record of success since you first started producing whatever you are preparing to promote. What's more, you've somehow effectively dealt with core issues that will continue to be important to you. Whether you know it or not, you've been honing the skills you need for promotions. Along the way, you've had to ask yourself many of the same questions that will be raised when it comes to publicity.

Of course, it's scary when you really aren't certain about the answers. It's like that for most everyone. However, it's often empowering to learn that no other person has the passion to promote or publicize what you do better than you. In fact, passion and a can-do attitude will get you further than anything else, including knowledge, skill, and even sheer luck.

But real knowledge helps. You can start by learning the basics.

Question Two: *"Can I Learn the Basics Fast Enough?"*

Yes, you can. It's as simple as this: When planning your PR, you'll discover that there are two basic considerations—there's the big picture and there's the little picture.

The big picture is about strategy. It charts the broad areas of your promotional concerns, scoping out the long range plans for where you'll go and why you want to get there. It's kind of like a page in an atlas that shows the overall layout of the country without too many details. You need it.

The little picture is like a detailed road map. This road map is equally important. You need it, too.

At first glance, they may seem like the same thing, but when you get lost or turned around, you'll discover firsthand that the difference between the big picture and the little picture is critical.

Why? It's all about the right tools to meet the goals you choose. Try to find your way out of the heart of a city using an atlas when you really need street-by-street driving instructions. Or try to figure out a strategic way to make it across the nation armed only with the street maps for each city you'll encounter on the way. If you are stuck with one PR planning tool when you need the other, you'll curse the difference between big picture and little picture, the atlas and road map.

At key points in the promotional process, too many details will overburden you and, at other times, lack of detail will undermine your efforts. When you are developing strategy, the atlas perspective is required. When you're implementing strategy, the road map perspective is necessary.

Understanding the best choice of tools for each phase in your journey can make all things possible. This book was created to provide both sets of tools, to help you understand the difference between the two, and to guide you through the necessary action of shifting gears back and forth between the two without losing momentum.

As you try to develop your atlas and your map, three basic elements must be integrated into both planning tools. The basics of all good promotional plans come right back to three simple areas: who, what, and when.

Who is your audience?

Real people are your audience. And, real people really matter. People are the heart of good PR. Publicity is done best when it's done for people for the right reasons. The power of PR can forever change lives—including your own—for the better. Build your PR mission on the belief that what you do or what you sell will help people and that it is important that they learn about it.

- Who needs to know about what you do?
- How will knowing about your products and services help them?
- Why do you care if they care?

Wrestle that information to the ground and come to terms with the answers. When your promotions are focused, the response you get back from the world will amaze you. Your job is to target your promotional efforts to the specific people who need your products or services. You'll reach them with the help of the media, but don't waste time on media venues that don't provide substantial access to your key markets.

What will you say?

Articulate your message with clarity. You must be able to consistently tell people who you are and what you do—simply and clearly. When possible, tell them with passion, style, and enthusiasm, but simply and clearly will be good enough to get the results you need. Focus on venues that will allow you to deliver your message, rather than taking anything you can get.

Have ready short answers for these questions:

- What do you do?
- Why do people need this?
- What makes you or your product different?

If you struggle over coming up with answers to these questions and come to the conclusion that they don't apply to your specific product or service, think again. And think harder this time.

For example, if you write fiction, maybe people need your product to provide an entertaining escape from the stress of their everyday worlds through a great laugh, a romantic thrill, or an armchair adventure. If you design beaded bracelets, perhaps you are helping women express their personal style or to make a unique fashion statement. If you are a personal chef, your services may help individuals with special diet needs or help working parents preserve the traditional family dinner.

Frame what you do and who you are around how you impact others.

When is the right time to speak up?

Timing can launch you or derail you. Consider timing strategically. Don't quite understand? Think this over: You open a new car wash in the harshest winter in Midwest history; cars won't line up. You try to sell snow shoes in the dog days of summer; nobody will be interested. On the first Monday in December, you try to arrange a book-signing event to promote your book during the holiday rush; the book chains tell you they don't have any room for events in December and they booked their January events back in October.

Timing can quick-track you or derail you. Get it right. If you don't know the seasons of your industry, you need to find these out from someone who does know.

Ask these questions of folks in your arena who are in-the-know:

- What time of year is the busiest?
- What time of year is the slowest?
- What deadlines are too important for me to miss?
- When would people be most receptive to my message?

Question Three: *"Yeah, Right, But Can I Really Do This?"*

Yes, you can. A commonly overlooked factor in your ultimate success is the need to care about how you handle your own emotions during the promotional process. Your feelings impact your success. How you feel about what you're doing is often more important than anything else, frequently more important than what you know and even who you know.

Your attitude can make or break you. You're a human, after all.

So, take care of your attitude by nurturing your feelings. Here are some of the feelings that are universally experienced by PR seekers:

- **"I'm anxious."**

That's normal. Anxiety frequently occurs when you don't know what to expect. Sometimes choosing ignorance is the more blissful path, but usually the best course is to learn what to expect and proactively prepare. When you feel anxious, ask yourself, "Who can help me prepare? What can I do to be prepared?"

- **"I'm afraid."**

That's normal. Most PR fears are about the possibility that you can not handle what may happen. If your expectation is that you must handle everything perfectly; lower those expectations now. Perfection is not the standard by which success is measured in this arena.

Showing up and enduring whatever comes your way gets the passing grade. Making a messy, awkward, and even clumsy attempt to deal with whatever lands in your lap moves you right up the scale toward expert.

When you are afraid, ask yourself, "If this were a situation that received a grade, what would it take to earn an 'A' and a 'C'? What would it take to really receive an 'F'?"

• "I'm confused."

That's normal. At first, you may be confused by everything happening around you. But, don't miss out on what's really going on. Typically, the most important changes are occurring within you. That is, the environment you're in may be changing, but, usually, so are you. When you are confused about things, ask yourself, "Who could help me see this situation from a better perspective?"

• "I'm suffering from stage fright."

That's so normal. Performance anxiety affects almost everyone, from the beginner to the most seasoned professional. The whole mess can often be avoided quite simply by being prepared, training yourself to stay on track, and learning positive self-talk techniques that don't sabotage your self-esteem. Be nice to yourself and don't discourage or belittle yourself. Never tell yourself things you wouldn't say aloud to a close friend. Tune in to your inner dialogue, listen, and ask yourself, "What would I say to someone else in similar circumstances?"

• "I'm stressed."

Normal, too. Sometimes stress can motivate you; sometimes it can handicap you. Different people have different reactions. If you fall into the first category, you must learn to control your stress before it controls you. The goal is to learn how to practice safe stress. Ask yourself, "What really counts here? How can I refocus my energy toward something I can control?"

The emotions listed above are only some of the feelings you may experience. As things happen, you may be stunned by your sometimes relaxed, sometimes heart-pounding responses to the mundane process of promotion. The sooner you recognize how valuable your feelings are, the sooner you will understand how your feelings can help you succeed.

Let yourself have fun, and you'll find opportunities that you never knew existed. Embrace the promotional process as a worthwhile adventure that is creative and intriguing, and you won't have to look for opportunities at all because opportunities will find you.

Doing PR right means that you will meet exciting people, develop your talents, grow your career, and help change a corner of the world. The PR tools and promotional resources you need are already within your reach, or soon can be.

Get ready! You're about to make some major PR breakthroughs.

COACHING CLINIC #1

Make a quick assessment of where you are in the PR process. Discover which barriers are holding you back and what factors are moving you forward. Then, do something about it.

Think about this: Is something holding you down or lifting you up?

Consider the downward pointing arrow:

- What forces are holding you down?
- What is stopping you?
- What is the roadblock in your way?
- What is too big for you to overcome?

Now, consider the upward arrow:

- What elements are lifting you up?
- Who is on your side?
- What's one thing that keeps helping you through?
- What and who have helped you get this far?

Okay, so what are you going to do about it? What can you do to reduce the number of barriers to success? What can you do to fortify or multiply the people or factors helping you through it all?

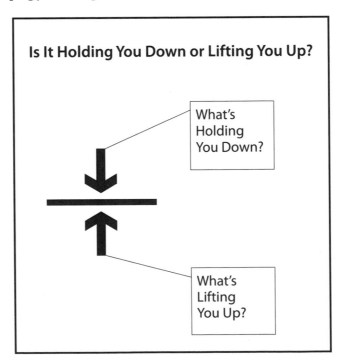

June Clark is the founding partner of Get There Media (GetThereMedia.com), a promotions and brand development company helping individuals and emerging businesses expand outreach and gain recognition in their field. She suggests the following:

- **Think outside the box.** Try to give a new spin to a tried-and-true tactic. Prospects are attracted to a blend of the familiar with a touch of something innovative.

- **Hone your matchmaking skills.** Who do you know who can help? Who has the leads to your market or contacts that you need? What strategic alliances with other parties or companies might you form that can give you a stronger identity or greater outreach? Don't be shy about asking everyone and anyone you know for anything. Often, that old cliché, "It's not what you know, but who," is true!

- **Be creative, catchy, fun.** Promoting yourself (or your product or business) should be enjoyable. You know yourself and your business better than anyone—be energized and bring as much joy and creativity to the process as possible…others will get caught up in your enthusiasm and respond similarly.

SESSION TWO
Shift Happens:
Letting Go and Moving Up

"I wish more people knew what I do...."
"I wish I could find better opportunities...."
"I wish I could sell more products and services...."

Everybody else is getting into the newspapers, into magazines, on the radio, and even on Oprah. Meanwhile, you've been so busy doing what you love and believing that the money would somehow follow that you've become accustomed to paying the light bill with your credit card, using paper plates for post-it notes, and wondering which will come first—your big break or your big breakdown.

For some reason, the promotional opportunities that you seem to attract are eating up more time than you can afford to spend, and the kind of attention you're getting really doesn't seem to be helping you as much as you need it to. You hate to sound ungrateful but you think—no, you *know*—that you genuinely deserve some serious media attention, not more of the same-old-same-old. Something has got to change and, quite frankly, it seems like it's going to have to be you.

When you come to this fork in the PR trail, the truth is you can stop where you are or take a leap of faith and change your life forever.

Take the leap.

By now, you know that your attitude can make or break you. And, you also know that applying the most basic efforts toward building your promotional platform can actually produce spectacular results. All that's left is shifting your gears into the willingness-to-change mode.

It's time to let go and move up—personally, professionally, and most of all, promotionally.

Resisting the need to change can undermine your success before you get started. So, before this big couch trip session is over, you need to recognize that you will have to make some changes to achieve and acquire the bigger changes you want and need. What's more, you've got to get ready to instigate changes, not just adapt to the ones that happen to you.

How?

Do the prep work.

Before you start making phone calls, pitching story ideas, and saying yes to the next so-called promotional opportunity, you have to lay the groundwork for doing PR right. If you are going to go to all the trouble of promoting who you are and what you do, it stands to good reason that you need to go about it in a smart way that allows every effort you make to act as a foundational brick toward your overall success.

Here's the Plan.

Just like painting the inside of your home, where choosing paint, organizing paintbrushes, taping off trim, and covering the carpet with a drop cloth is just as important as the actual painting itself, PR prep work is as necessary as the promoting itself. In fact, it is vital.

And, what's more, doing prep work empowers your potential to transcend way beyond promotional success. The more you know about what you really need to know, the better equipped you will be to succeed in every corner of the marketplace. Your success on every level increases when you understand what your promotional options are and when you can choose from an array of choices rather than try to follow a rote series of how-to instructions.

The next step is to choose a goal that you can visualize in your mind.

How do you do that?

It's a simple framing issue. Instead of fixating on the limited idea *I want to do this list of things*, reframe the goal to be *I want to go where I can have this and I can do that*. It's sort of like painting a room in your house. You'll be more satisfied with the results if you focus on the serene environment that you want to ultimately create (your goal destination) rather than becoming fixated on a paint can of seafoam green no matter what (a limited idea).

So, start with a destination: You need to get to the place where you can acquire recognition for what you do and who you are.

Whether you're just starting out or you've been at this thing you do for many seasons, the process of moving toward that place you need to be is choreographed in three steps:

- Plan
- Tools
- Action

Your plan

Make no mistake, your plan is to get to that place where you are recognized for who you are and what you do. What does that place look like? A compelling vision about your destination can guide and motivate you to make the small and large changes that will help you reach your goal destination faster.

The rest of this book will help you fill in the step-by-step blanks to get there. You will learn how to steadily build your promotional strategy. Warning signs will be posted so you can avoid the pitfalls. Rescue techniques will be illustrated in case you make a misstep. To make your plan work for yourself, you must steadily gather facts and information about your unique destination, that which you need and want. Then, you will use that info to collect the required tools for your success.

Your tools

As your plan becomes clearer, you will know exactly what specific tools you will need to implement your plan. Later, this book will help you design custom communication tools like press kits, press releases, and more that you will use in your promotion. However, three stock tools of the trade are offered now. These tools are conceptual techniques that will help you make decisions and set successful strategies in motion along the way.

Tool of the Trade #1: The "How-Big-Is-Big?" PR Measuring Stick

This tool can save you from disappointment and misunderstanding in the PR world and beyond. It is designed to address expectations.

It is often a hard lesson to learn that what you expect and what the world expects can be very different. They say that beauty is in the eye of the beholder. Most often, expectations of success, great work, fast turnarounds, big money, and big names (and what constitutes too much stress, but that's for another time) are also in the eye of the beholder.

You can reduce misunderstandings and disappointments by making sure you and those you interact with are on the same playing field.

The solution is as simple as asking. Ask: How big is big? Find out if it is six inches or six feet. Ask: How much money is big money? Is it $6,000 or $6 million? Ask: How quick is a fast turnaround? Is it six hours or six days? Ask: Whom do you consider a "big" name? Is it the local mayor or the vice president of the United States?

Ask—never assume your measuring stick is the same as the rest of the world's.

Tool of the Trade #2: The PR Chalk Line

Don't overlook the incredible value of drawing a line. Place a deliberate red mark between what you *could do* and what you *will do*. Sharp boundaries help you survive the soul-searching sessions when you must sort out what's working…and *for whom.*

If you don't already have clearly defined boundaries, set some preliminary ones. For example, maybe you won't fly, or you won't launch a speaking career while the kids are little, or you won't miss your morning jog, or you won't work for less than peanuts or caviar.

Not sure where the line belongs? That's why you draw it in chalk, not permanent marker. You can always make changes when you need to. It's just much easier to reset boundaries or adopt more realistic standards when some initial parameters exist.

Start by defining a solid, measurable limit on how many hours you can and will do PR work on a monthly basis. Set a clear limit on how much time and money any one project is worth. Make a clear evaluation regarding your return on investment—in PR, it is how well any particular event allows you to connect with your target audience—before you allot valuable resources.

Tool of the Trade #3: The PR Scales of Personal Justice

You'll have an opportunity to use this tool repeatedly. Don't be afraid to weigh the pros and the cons of your PR opportunities. There's no personal justice in wearing yourself out chasing things that offer no value toward reaching your goals.

It is possible to readily discern what is worth your efforts and what your efforts are truly worth. Seek some balance.

Here are some ideas on how to weigh the opportunities that may turn up:

- Determine if the cost of your time and resources to be involved in a project outweigh the project's ultimate value to you. How do you figure this? It stands to reason that if you are not getting paid, you are volunteering. When you give away your time, figure your time is worth just above the national average of any volunteer's time. For the past few years that value has been estimated at about $20 an hour. If your involvement is "costing" you $20 an hour, does that expense outweigh its potential value to you? If you regularly charge more than $20 per hour, use that figure.
- If you are learning something that you believe is worthwhile and you are growing because of your involvement in a particular opportunity, consider this: What would it cost you to hire someone to teach you the same info?
- What is the "wow" value of the experience as an addendum to your bio or resume?
- At the end of a long week or at the end of a long life, what is the feel-good value?
- If it's media exposure that you're making a decision about, consider what this same media charges for an ad in its publication or commercial time on its program. Getting a story about you in a magazine or being interviewed on a radio or TV program is intrinsically worth more than paid advertisement, but knowing the advertising rate allows you to consider some baseline for deciding if it is worth it. However, appearing in a publication or on a show that doesn't reach the audience you need to reach won't help. If you don't already know who the audience is for this particular media, ask your contact

or call their sales department for a copy of their sales literature, which should clarify who they perceive their audience to be.

Plan, tools...*action!*

Getting where you want to go requires action. Nobody is going to drag you to the place you belong. It's up to you. The best plans and the finest tools don't achieve desired results unless action is applied.

Don't allow yourself to get stuck. Force progress.

The rest of this book suggests specific actions you'll need to take to achieve specific results. Still, it does help to realize that there's more to taking action than simply responding to how-to prompts. Here are four actions that are important to recognize as bona fide options along the PR path:

PR Action Option #1: You Can Say "No."

Every time you have a chance to make clear decisions about what's next—be willing to say "no" to those clients, projects, and possibilities that are outside the scope of your passion, your expertise, or your time availability. Everyone's energy is limited. Use your energy to leverage everything you've got to move you upward.

Learning to focus requires saying "no" to some things at some times. However, "yes" is an option, too. Say "yes" to those opportunities that give you the most return on investment.

It's *not* all or nothing. You can pick and choose. Accept what you want; say "no" to the parts that don't work for you.

PR Action Option #2: You Can Let Go.

When things feel heavy, they probably are. Stop and take a minute to hear yourself when you start thinking, "I have to, but I wish I didn't...I need to, but I would rather not." *Should, ought, have-to* and *they expect* are often red flags to let go of emotional baggage.

When these words seep into your conversation or into your thoughts, it's a good time to remember to dump the junk from every level—personally and professionally. Take a clue from the airlines: too much baggage is a big problem.

Whatever your baggage is, you will come to a point when it's time to let go.

The weight of unneeded baggage weighs down your hope and happiness. It gets in the way of your professional development. When things feel difficult or heavy or personally exhausting, remember to ask yourself, "What part can I let go?"

PR Action Option #3: You Can Move on.

You can move on...and, you must move on.

One thing you can count on from a good PR journey is you will be exposed to new ideas, new landscapes, and new people. Sometimes, as you grow and change, your own environment will no longer be appropriate for who you are and who you are becoming.

At first, you may not grasp exactly what is transpiring. However, if you are in the wrong environment, it is common to feel crazy, stupid, retarded, or worthless. You may waste a lot of energy and time exploring whether the crazy, stupid, retarded, and worthless labels are accurate. Don't bother; the solution to the problem does not lie there.

Stop questioning how you feel. Accept your feelings as valid and focus on the wrong environment part of that scenario. When you are in the wrong environment, you feel wrong. Not because you're wrong, but because the environment is wrong—for you.

Sometimes your environment does not fit with who you are.

It's as if you unwittingly contributed a box full of rocks to the neighborhood rummage sale. Rocks in a box just aren't good rummage sale material. Carry that same bunch of rocks over to a rock show and it's a whole different scenario. Rock hounds may wildly appreciate what you've got.

PR Action Option #4: You Can Choose to Make a Difference.

Sometimes seeking publicity for your work or for yourself can feel self-serving and shallow. It can be and it is if you don't honestly believe that what you're doing is important or that it really makes a difference to others.

The truth is making a difference in the world matters. You can tell yourself it doesn't matter, and you can valiantly pretend it isn't the driving force, but underneath it all, making a difference is what makes things worthwhile. Along the way, you will have moments when you can choose a quick chance in the spotlight or a quiet spot somewhere far behind the scenes. Trust your heart and choose the option that you believe makes a difference. You won't ever be disappointed.

COACHING CLINIC #2

You want to get there—and it's possible. Here's a visualization exercise to help you identify the tangible goals that need to be achieved on the way from where you are to where you want to be. On the left hand side of a blank piece of paper, draw a small x to represent where you are. Across the page place a big X to represent that place where you want to go. It's time to get things moving.

The big X

Beside that big X (where you're going), place the answers to these three questions:

- What media—radio, TV, magazine, newspaper—will you have appeared in when you get there?

• How much money will you be making when you get there?
• What other projects or services will you have completed that will be ready to
  roll out by then?

The halfway there mark

Draw a horizontal line that connects the small x to the big X. Put a "½" symbol
to represent the halfway mark between the small x and the big X. As you think
about getting from here to there, don't forget that the halfway mark really matters.

It's a place to regroup. It's a spot to take a breath. It's where you can re-energize
and reevaluate. Ponder these questions:

• What should be completed by the time you get there?
• What will you need to make the second half of your journey?

The small x

Now back to the here and now. From where you are now, you must do certain
things to get yourself closer to the finish line. What could you do to take a few
steps toward your goals? Answer these three questions:

• What could you do today?
• What could you do by next week?
• What could you have done by a month from now?

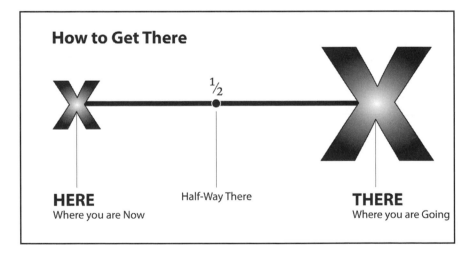

How to Get There

½

HERE
Where you are Now

Half-Way There

THERE
Where you are Going

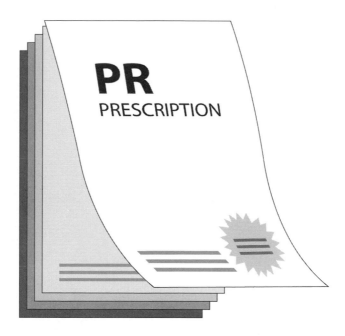

Here are some tips from Dan O'Day (DanOday.com), who coaches radio and television personalities around the world. As a public speaker, he's addressed audiences ranging from fifteen to 1,500 people in thirty-four different countries. He's also the author of *Personality Radio*, which has been referred to by radio professionals as "the DJ's bible."

- When you're on the radio, aside from knowing where your audience is (so you can mention the locale) and the focus of the program, don't worry about local, regional or demographic differences. The big difference is *you*. Focus your attention on delivering your message clearly, confidently, and convincingly.
- Contrary to the "I've got to customize each interview to match each radio audience" approach, all your interviews should sound very much the same. You don't need to worry about repetition; the audience who hears you on the Tulsa morning show will not also hear your appearance on the Omaha mid-day program.
- Being a guest is completely different than buying a commercial. The one advantage of a commercial is control: You determine exactly what will be said and how it will be communicated. But, your appearance as a guest confers upon you a credibility you (literally) cannot buy.

PHASE II

The Rx to Analyze Your Audience

For a long time, I thought everybody understood the importance of knowing your audience. I simply didn't know what *others* didn't know until I signed a deal with a publisher to represent a new imprint.

The situation grew more surreal by the minute. A real problem was potential mutiny on my own ship. My little team of creative brainiacs wanted to revolt before we even got started on the new project. They had me cornered at my desk with a copy of our signed contract, the first month's retainer, and the just-arrived list of the publisher's upcoming titles.

My team was startled by the title list. They wanted answers or they wanted out. "Robin, Robin, Robin...did you see this product list? Who could the target market possibly be? What in the world are they trying to do? How will they ever build any kind of company brand when the product list is so freaking scattered that just looking at their books makes you wonder who they are and what they do?"

I didn't have immediate answers. Confronted by the list of books, I, too, was a bit startled. What had sounded like a really cool collection when I chatted with the CEO now looked like a wild array of rogue titles. One book was a novel by a sci-fi writer, the rest were nonfiction tomes by a sex expert, a disillusioned nun, a retired trainer from an Army special units program, an expert on mythical monsters, and a bunch of others, each with richly unusual backgrounds and highly extraordinary stories.

"Well, yeah, I sort of see what you mean. But, the books, they each have their own audiences. That sex thing certainly has a great chance. And there's a ton of people who love the Loch Ness monster. And this Army special units deal is a really cool military operation, for Heaven's sake."

They implored me to look deeper. In this case, since the publisher was the client, part of our job was to help build its reputation in the marketplace—to define the publisher's image based on the books it published. By virtue of that fact, the line of books needed to be seen as a collection—a family of products—that would appeal to a certain kind of audience.

This family of books did not, at first glance, seem to be remotely related.

"Who is the audience? What kind of reader would pick up one book and then even dream of reading any other book the publisher offers? Where do we find groups of this-certain-kind-of-reader so we can tell them about all this stuff? Where is the pattern for even the slightest chance of repeat sales? Do you really think the average Loch Ness lover also needs enlightenment from a sex expert or a closer look at the Catholic church?"

Legitimate questions. Difficult answers.

Being a bunch of relentless overachievers, we worked our butts off on that project. I personally learned a ton about audience profiling, got some worthwhile media hits, and made friends with some of the most intriguing and intelligent people I ever hoped to meet. Today, when I talk about knowing your audience, the passion you'll hear in my voice was sparked here...with Martians, the Catholic Church, and, of course, Nessie, the Loch Ness monster.

SESSION THREE
Ready-or-Not Target Market

"I think my audience is anyone and everyone."

Now that you've looked inward and have rearranged lots of personal stuff, it's time to look outward and prepare to take on the part of the world that's equally important: *your target market.*

If you really want your promotional efforts to help generate the kind of awareness that directly impacts more sales of products and services, it's time to take a good, hard look at the people who buy what you sell.

Identifying your target market is the foundation for your success. You need to know this group of people in the same way a card player knows how to build a winning hand from a deck of cards.

Think about that.

The first time you were handed a deck of cards as a child, you didn't instantly recognize the difference between the cards or the suits. But, eventually it was possible to play Go Fish, Crazy Eights, and maybe even poker.

Your target market customers are like those cards and your strategies are often like switching gears by playing different games with the same set of fifty-two cards.

You need to be able to deftly choose and regroup the cards and start different games without getting confused. Poker is different than Go Fish. The cards look the same, but they must be played differently. In a similar way, at certain stages in PR, you need to organize your prospects in very different ways. You need to know your particular game rules, be able to recognize your targets when you spot them, and proactively do your part to attain your goals.

As you get clear about who your target market is, you will naturally become more insightful about how and where to focus your publicity, marketing, and sales efforts.

So, let's get to know this new "deck of cards."

Who Is Your Target Market?

Like every card in the deck, every person in the world has potential. In reality, it is probably true that the whole world could or should appreciate what you do. So, it is natural to imagine that your consumer base is virtually everybody. After all, in your line of work, in your field of business, you could help anyone and everyone— every card in the deck, so to speak.

But you shouldn't. Thinking that everyone is your target market is like playing cards without realizing that managing the cards strategically could help you win. You have the potential to win here, but you need to play your cards right. Your first step is realizing precisely why and how you really need to narrow down the scope.

Narrow down?

The concept can seem disconcerting at first.

You may think: "I don't want to exclude anyone. I don't want any restrictions or limitations around choosing my customers or clients. I just want to leave things wide open and see what happens. I want everyone." You may even take a closer look at what you're doing and think: "My stuff really is different. Everyone really does need what I have. I've built the proverbial better mousetrap. I'm ready and waiting for the world to beat a path to my door. That's what I want: the world."

That means *everyone*. Right?

Not quite.

Take a closer look at that build-a-better-mousetrap scenario. It's *exactly* what we're talking about. The rarely considered part of that timeless wisdom is that it's not everyone who shows up at your door. All those people who are showing up to buy the better mousetrap actually have something terribly important in common. They all have rodent problems. People without a mouse problem aren't standing in line for a better mousetrap. These folks aren't buying last year's mousetrap, either. They aren't even thinking of mousetraps. It's not an appropriate buying season for them *until* they have a need to rid themselves of mice.

Why does any of that matter to you?

It's critical to understand that *everyone* in the world is not part of your target market. In fact, it's not about wanting everyone—it's really about *not wanting* everyone. So, before you lump clients and customers into one faceless group of everybody, consider this: The everyone mindset will undermine your promotional efforts and block opportunities for your success.

Why?

The everyone mindset puts you in passive mode. You're waiting for them to choose you, instead of doing your part to connect with exactly who you do want.

The truth is you have to define who you want. You simply do not have the luxury of treating everyone as if they were exactly the same. They aren't the same. Some are ready to buy; some are not. Of course, it's great that you have a better solution to a universal problem. It's wonderful that virtually everyone may eventually need what you do, but it's best to recognize that everyone's needs are on different timing cycles.

You can't control their circumstances, but you can take ownership of yours. You must find ways to manage your time and efforts carefully or you'll wear yourself out spouting the merits of mousetraps to people who have not yet encountered a mouse.

It's time to focus on people who can help cultivate your success. The sooner you understand that everyone is not your customer, the sooner your success can grow and stabilize.

How do you figure out who's who?

Like cards, at first observation, it may be hard to distinguish the different suits of people. Start narrowing down your reach by placing some qualifying factors around your real prospects that distinguish them from the crowd.

Focus first on people who are ready right now to employ your services or buy your product.

It's ready-or-not time.

Who are your ready-right-now folks? If you were selling mousetraps, your ready-right-now buyers would be the ones who have serious mouse trouble. Mice are in the house, droppings are in the pantry, a live one just scared the bejeebies out of Grandma. These buyers are motivated to end the mouse madness now.

You aren't selling mousetraps, but every product or service has ready-right-now people. Ready-right-now prospects are ready to buy a product or pay for a service today, next week, or within the next month. They're the

Sylvia's Passion

Sylvia Mendoza is the award-winning author of *The Book of Latina Women: 150 Vidas (Lives) of Passion, Strength and Success*. In her book, Sylvia highlights the contributions of 150 remarkable Latinas—from fiery superstars who blazed new trails in pop culture to little-known heroes whose brave actions changed history.

Using her book as the central theme for her professional platform, Sylvia has built a cohesive career that immerses her in the work she loves most: reaching as many women and girls as possible, in order to inspire and empower them. By defining her audience and clarifying her personal mission, Sylvia has found it easier to recognize opportunities and make important career choices along the way. That's how she wound up volunteering at the San Diego Juvenile Hall as a bookclub facilitator for young women living there.

And, that's why she began teaching a writing workshop for Osher Lifelong Learning Institute at California State University, San Marcos, where she was recognized as a "Woman of Distinction" for her contributions in promoting awareness of gender issues.

One of the most important parts of her creative career unfolded naturally when she began utilizing her book as a marketing tool to launch her speaking career. By actively focusing her work on her passion, Sylvia and her motivational speeches and workshops caught the attention of the National Women's History Project, which invited her to speak at Sonoma State University. Sylvia's lecture was covered by C-Span's Book TV for National Women's History month.

Mendoza's passion continues to inspire and motivate women and girls nationwide.

PR Tip: Focus on your passion. Seek out ways to volunteer and to work with like-minded groups which share enthusiasm for your mission and have built an audience that overlaps with your target market.

customers or clients who have a need that is urgent enough that they want to do something about it now. They're motivated to act, to buy, to do something immediately.

What should you do with them?

Make it easy to be found when they are ready. Your promotional goal is to make the path to your door smoother to navigate and your door as easy as possible to find. Think about that. If they don't knock on your door asking to buy stuff, you have to be a field salesman and wander around knocking on their doors. It's much cheaper and much easier to do what it takes to make it simple for them to come to you than it is for you to pack up and go track them down one sale at a time.

Here are some things you can do:

- Focus on their needs.
- Help them find answers to their right-now problems.
- Share information on who you are and what you can do for them right now.
- Be direct. Cut to the chase.
- Expedite their waiting time.
- Do the business card thing. Having business cards is one thing; handing them out to everyone everywhere makes it easier for people to contact you.
- Put a signature at the end of all your e-mails: name, phone number, website.

And, of course, do everything you can to anticipate when your customers will have seasons of need. Connect the dots between ready-right-now needs and your ready-right-now solutions. Take care of the folks who are ready-right-now as fast as possible by selling them your product or service. Don't make them wait in line behind probably-someday people.

Who Are the Probably-Someday People?

Probably-someday prospects aren't ready to buy a product or service for at least a few months. They are not ready now. A little farther down the road, maybe four to twelve months from now, they will be ready. They just don't have an immediate need. To revisit the mousetrap analogy, these folks don't have an official mouse problem yet. They may know their neighbor has mice. They may wonder: "What caused the hole in my dog food bag?" But, they don't believe there's a reason to take action—yet.

What should you do with them?

Make it easy for current and past customers and clients to tell a friend about you. A big part of doing what it takes in your smoother-path, easier-to-find-door efforts is making it simple for your clients and customers to refer others to you.

The early rounds of customers who understand why you're so great will naturally help widen the path to your door. They will often do valuable legwork, spreading the word about you to others who need to know who you are.

Here are some things you can do:

- Be neighborly. Show you care. Remember that being nice really matters.
- Ask your contacts for referrals and introductions to others you could help.
- Explain how you or your product help people who have certain sorts of needs or who find themselves in certain kinds of situations.
- Know the early warning signs for problems others face which you can resolve, or for needs that you can satisfy.
- Explain to people how the solutions you offer can allow them to avoid potential problems.
- Position yourself as the go-to guy or the go-to gal for the moment when probably-someday becomes ready-right-now—the moment that strange hole in the dog food bag is revealed for what it is, a rodent problem.

Make sure your messages address the needs of the probably-someday crowd, but keep your priorities focused on helping the ready-right-now customer or client.

Who Are the Maybe-Never People?

Maybe-never people are individuals who probably won't buy a product or service in the next twelve to fourteen months. Because their possible purchase is so far from now, they fall into the maybe-never category. Sure, they may come around…but odds are many of them won't. In fact, they may never be interested in your services or products. They may simply have no need. Or, they may prefer a different way to resolve their needs than through your products or services. They might even prefer to live with their problems. Or maybe they can not afford your products or services.

What should you do about them?

It is safe to set most of these people on the back shelf and not worry about them. Just understand that they may change or their circumstances may change. If they change, you need to be ready to deal with them then. That is, when they climb down from the shelf and transport themselves into probably-someday territory, you need to know it and pay attention to them. Until that happens, you simply can't afford to waste time and energy trying to win them over.

Their conditions and their circumstances are genuinely out of your control.

But, *yours* are not. You can make an impact on your own situation by choosing where to focus. So, focus on your bottom line.

To succeed, you have to focus on the people who will buy products or services right now or probably someday soon. And don't forget, they need you every bit as much as you need them.

So get strategic:

Ready or Not?	**Figure it out...**
	My product is: _____ My service is: _____

Ready-Right-Now Prospects are ready to buy a product or pay for a service today, next week, or within the next month.	**Ready-Right-Now** • Who needs what you have today...next week...or within the next month? • What is happening in *their* life that caused them to need *your* product or service now? • What problems can your product or service resolve immediately? • What can you do *now* to make them aware that you have what they need?
Probably-Someday... Soon Prospects are not yet ready to buy a product or pay for a service for at least a few months, but probably within the next year.	**Probably-Someday...Soon** • Who eventually will need what you have—not immediately, but a little further out...within the next 4 to 6 months? • What will happen in *their* life that will cause them to need *your* product or service? • What problems can you prevent from happening? • What can you do to make them think of you as soon as they realize that they need what you can provide?
Maybe-Never...Ever Prospects may never be interested. They have reasons that prevent them from being interested (or they lack reasons that could motivate them to be interested) in buying a product or paying for a service.	**Maybe-Never...Ever** • What groups of people fall within the parameters of your target market but can reasonably be eliminated as prospects? • What factors exist that make it possible to predict that they can be ruled out as being likely prospects? • What can you do to make sure you don't waste time trying to win over people who are not likely to buy your products or services this year?

Paul Stannard is the founder and CEO of SmartDraw.com, maker of SmartDraw, the world's most popular business graphics software. He listened and learned from his customers:

When we first started out, from time to time we used to sit around and argue about how our customers perceived our product. Like every company, we wanted to know why our customers picked us instead of our biggest rival.

One day we came up with a brilliant idea: *"Why don't we ask them?"*

When we really started talking to our customers, we were completely surprised to find out that most of them had never even heard of our rival's product. They weren't choosing our product over somebody else's product. They were choosing our product instead of paper and pencil.

Ask your customers why they chose you. Communicating with our customers has become the most important part of our success.

The Hardcores and the Newbies of Your Field

"My whole approach to PR skyrocketed when I finally realized that promoting is as easy as finding a mentor who believes in me…or being a mentor to someone who just wants to be shown the ropes."

By now, you recognize that the people you want to focus on most are the people who are ready or nearly ready to buy your products or services. Ready to get started?

Pull some key winning cards from the everyone pool. In the same way you might pluck all the aces out of a randomly shuffled deck, you need to identify and gather up the members of the target market that are most important to your success—your *Hardcores*. Every subject, every genre, every product, and every service has its own group of people who are Hardcores—and, yours does, too.

Your Hardcores

How do you recognize *your* Hardcores in the big group of everybody who might want to buy your products and services? You train yourself to see them. Just like seeing the aces in a deck of cards.

Here's what they look like. Your Hardcores are very focused people…focused on your field or topic. They know and use the industry-specific terms and jargon of your field. They are usually interested in adding new depth or dimension to their considerable knowledge base. They have a deep understanding and love for your chosen topic. Some have made it their business to know all there is to know about the field that you are in. They rest high above the sphere of general interest.

Every field has a group of Hardcores. In your own life, you encounter Hardcores from multiple fields every day. They're the geeks of their chosen field—

whether the particular field is geeky or not—in fact, the field could be football, high fashion, fishing, theater, or anything. Hardcore veterans are defined by their pursuit of substantial, expert-level knowledge in their field of interest.

For example, if the topic is the music of the Beatles, the Hardcores would know such things as what order the Fab Four's albums were released, the lyrics to even the obscure songs, and who sang lead when and why. Take them to a Beatle Fan Fest and they know what's new, what's common, what's unique—and they don't get confused or thrilled without reason. They are the ones who care about getting deeply involved in the extreme details of their part of the world.

But, Hardcores are not just music or entertainment fans. If the topic is mental illness, that topic's Hardcore audience would know information like the difference between schizophrenia, bipolar disorder, and OCD. They'd probably know about movies like *A Beautiful Mind* and *One Flew Over the Cuckoo's Nest*, and whether Bob Newhart played a psychiatrist or a psychologist on his classic television series.

Hardcores may work, play, or just enjoy knowing about their chosen topic, but they really know their stuff. If you are selling coffee, your coffee-loving Hardcore customer has taste-tested nearly every coffee product and can describe and compare flavors like a food critic.

Your Hardcore audience is unique to you.

Don't worry if it seems a little difficult to identify these folk at first. Just like when you first learned to play a simple card game, initially you may mistake a different card in the deck for an ace, or a different person in the target market for a Hardcore.

From a universal standpoint, there's no specific age required to qualify an individual as a Hardcore. There's also no specific academic standing, no financial level, no set IQ, and no height requirement. What makes a Hardcore a Hardcore, what really defines them, is all about their level of interest in, understanding of, and experience with the particular topic at hand.

So, if you're selling trading cards, your Hardcore customers may be a game-playing fifth-grader and a forty-year-old collector who both know one specific brand of trading cards better than the company that manufactured them. If you are teaching people to knit, your Hardcores may be teenagers, new moms, and even great-grandparents, all who simply know and love yarn, dyes, and the differences between knitting styles.

If you're writing mysteries, your Hardcore readers may be men or women, old or young, married or single, but they will all know mystery authors, the different subcategories of mystery novels, and the real reasons they can't get enough of this sort of entertainment.

Somewhere out there, your own chosen topic has a group of Hardcores. This group is extremely important to you and—even better—you are extremely important to them.

Here's why you are important: Your Hardcores have or know about a big need in your field. They think about this quite a lot. Sometimes it keeps them up late at night. Sometimes it wakes them up early in the morning. They want this big need resolved and you have the power to help resolve it for them.

What is their need?

That's where you come in.

Hardcores have needs you can resolve.

In no uncertain terms, you must intimately understand their problems, needs, and wants because you have products or services that will help them. You may be able to fill their unquenchable thirst for a certain type of entertainment, or resolve a problem that changes their daily lives, or prevent an issue that threatens to occur or reoccur, or bring new information and ideas to help them see things from a fresh and important perspective, or even change how they perceive themselves or how others perceive them.

Think about what specific expertise and experience you can offer this part of your target market. Hardcores reasonably expect you to know and understand their needs and desires. Most will not expect you to know every nuance of the industry, but they will want you to be engaged in it. The greater your level of understanding of both your industry and your Hardcores, the more magnetic you will become to them.

When you know why your Hardcore community is interested in you and your work, your promotional efforts can be transformed into clean, clear, direct messages that can positively impact and expedite the growth of your success.

You just need to figure out what to say and then say it. Articulate who you are and what you do in a way that is meaningful to this specific target audience. Do more than speak the language of your industry. Master the language, and be fluent in the lingo.

Your Hardcores won't respond to general talk. They respond only when they feel you are talking directly to them about their individual interests.

So you need to know a few important things.

How will your Hardcores use your product or service? How can you help them accomplish their goals or meet their needs this year, quarter, month, week, or between coffee breaks? How can your products or services help put control in their hands? How do you reach them? How could you reach them better? How can you target and reach more just like them?

Be aware of the media your target audience is most likely to see and hear. Read what your Hardcores read. Where do they gather their decision-making information? Do they hang out on the Internet? Do they read newspapers? Do they read magazines? Do they watch TV or listen to radio? You need to know.

Connect. Connecting with Hardcores is vitally important because these people share a valuable key that opens many doors for your success. These folks routinely act as mentors in your field. They are often uniquely qualified to help you reduce your own learning curves in record time or to connect others to you if they believe you can help.

COACHING CLINIC #4a

Your Hardcores can single-handedly make your promotional efforts profitable. Start here and now by creating a preliminary fact sheet about your unique Hardcore audience—your most valuable market niche. Answer a series of easy questions to tack down hard information on who they are, what they need, how to reach them, and what you need to tell them about your products and services. Then, focus on cultivating your target market, connecting yourself or your products to this community.

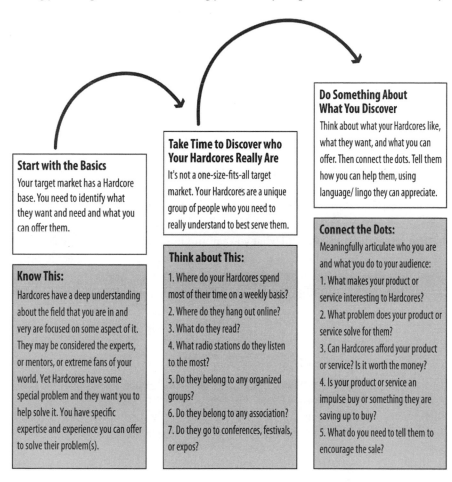

Start with the Basics

Your target market has a Hardcore base. You need to identify what they want and need and what you can offer them.

Know This:

Hardcores have a deep understanding about the field that you are in and very are focused on some aspect of it. They may be considered the experts, or mentors, or extreme fans of your world. Yet Hardcores have some special problem and they want you to help solve it. You have specific expertise and experience you can offer to solve their problem(s).

Take Time to Discover who Your Hardcores Really Are

It's not a one-size-fits-all target market. Your Hardcores are a unique group of people who you need to really understand to best serve them.

Think about This:

1. Where do your Hardcores spend most of their time on a weekly basis?
2. Where do they hang out online?
3. What do they read?
4. What radio stations do they listen to the most?
5. Do they belong to any organized groups?
6. Do they belong to any association?
7. Do they go to conferences, festivals, or expos?

Do Something About What You Discover

Think about what your Hardcores like, what they want, and what you can offer. Then connect the dots. Tell them how you can help them, using language/ lingo they can appreciate.

Connect the Dots:

Meaningfully articulate who you are and what you do to your audience:
1. What makes your product or service interesting to Hardcores?
2. What problem does your product or service solve for them?
3. Can Hardcores afford your product or service? Is it worth the money?
4. Is your product or service an impulse buy or something they are saving up to buy?
5. What do you need to tell them to encourage the sale?

Your Newbies

But what about the rest of the cards in the deck? You've taken time to train yourself to recognize your Hardcores, but if you really want more influence and higher sales, you must recognize and address the next most important segment of your audience—your *Newbies*.

To continue the card game analogy, you've already removed the aces. It's time now to pick out the jacks, the queens, and the kings that represent your Newbies.

Every topic has a Newbie following. Your Newbies are the group of newcomers who recently arrived on your turf. They're inexperienced in your world of expertise, but they're full of fresh enthusiasm and curiosity. They want or need to learn more about your area, which, to them, is a new corner of the world.

Whatever field you are in, your Newbies are people who are learning the ropes, looking for friendly mentors, and interested in any information that is helpful in their starting-out stage. Everything, even a basic concept, may be fresh and new to them.

For example, Newbie cooks are excited about cooking food, but they don't yet know all the fancy kitchen tools or the difference between terms like braise and sauté. So if you've got culinary products and services, put on your mentoring hat and share what you know.

But Newbies aren't just found in the culinary arts arena. Newbie parents are the ones who will buy a trunk full of baby stuff for their newborn's first planned outing and lug everything around for every expedition because they don't yet know if they (and the child) can survive without every gadget they can afford to buy.

Just remember to be careful what you say and how much you say. The Newbies of any topic usually only have an entry-level knowledge of their specific topic. Some have only a limited interest in the subject. Information that is too technical or too deep can be difficult for them to consume. When you talk over their heads or out of their interest zones, you risk losing their attention. Yet, when you provide information relevant to their needs, their response is immediate—they buy into who you are and what you're promoting and selling.

Why take the time to know these people? The size of this niche is significant—there are more Newbies out there than you may suspect. Newbies typically outnumber Hardcores by about twelve to one. Knowing your market niche helps you determine the best ways to effectively communicate with them. Identify and cultivate the members of your Newbie niche and your success is guaranteed.

COACHING CLINIC #4b

Create a preliminary fact sheet about your unique Newbie audience. Answer a series of easy questions to tack down hard information on who they are, what they need, where to reach them, and what you need to tell them about your products and services.

Now think about this. It's easy to identify the distinguishing characteristics when you're sorting cards, but when you're working with real customers and clients, you'll soon discover that it's a little harder to tell them apart. The dividing line that separates one group from another may not seem so clear-cut in real life. In fact, the dividing line between Hardcores and Newbies can seem impossibly blurred.

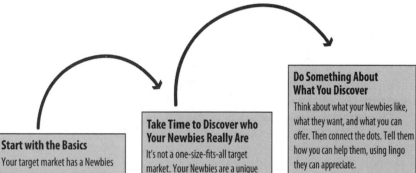

Do Something About What You Discover

Think about what your Newbies like, what they want, and what you can offer. Then connect the dots. Tell them how you can help them, using lingo they can appreciate.

Start with the Basics

Your target market has a Newbies base. You need to identify what they want and need and what you can offer them.

Take Time to Discover who Your Newbies Really Are

It's not a one-size-fits-all target market. Your Newbies are a unique group of people you need to understand so you can best serve them.

Connect the Dots:

Meaningfully articulate who you are and what you do to your audience:
1. What makes your product or service interesting to Hardcores?
2. What problem does your product or service solve for them?
3. Can Hardcores afford your product or service? Is it worth the money?
4. Is your product or service an impulse buy or something they are saving up to buy?
5. What do you need to tell them to encourage the sale?

Know This about Newbies:

Your Newbies are newcomers who recently arrived on your scene. They are inexperienced, but full of enthusiasm. They want to learn more about your turf. Newbies have some special problems doing what they do and they want their problems solved.

You have specific expertise and experience you can offer to solve their problem(s).

Think about this:

1. Where do your Hardcores spend most of their time on a weekly basis?
2. Where do they hang out online?
3. What do they read?
4. What radio stations do they listen to the most?
5. Do they belong to any organized groups?
6. Do they belong to any association?
7. Do they go to conferences, festivals, or expos?

Hardcore or Newbie?

Some of your target market may seem well suited to either category. This is understandable when you realize that your Hardcore members were Newbies when they started out. They are all in the constant process of changing and growing.

You can fully expect to encounter some very experienced Newbies who are virtually transforming into underdeveloped Hardcores.

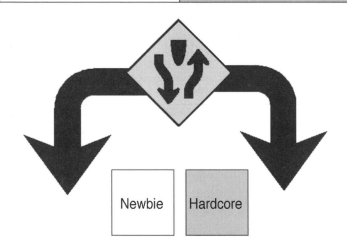

Newbies to the left...

Newbies share a relatively newfound or surface-level interest in what you are doing. By direct comparison to your Hardcores, Newbies have less knowledge of your area. However, they are interested in developing a better understanding and they have unique needs that you can fulfill.

But, how far left are they on the big scale?

Knowing the line between the two groups expedites promotions.

Hardcores to the right...

Your group of Hardcores share a deep understanding and love for what you are doing. In contrast to Newbies, they have a substantial, expert-level knowledge of your topic's area, and are interested in adding depth or dimension to what they already know. They have unique needs that you can fulfill.

But, how far right are they on the big scale?

Knowing the line between the groups helps you shift gears flawlessly.

Newbie   Hardcore

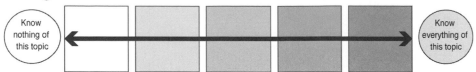

The Big Scale. Your definition of Newbies and Hardcores is relative to where you are in the process.

Know nothing of this topic

Know everything of this topic

Where is the line that declares official transformation? That's up to you to decide, but it is crucial for you to do so. As in a card game, you must know what card belongs where if you want to win.

Size people up quickly and decide where they belong in your process. You can't control who they are, but you can certainly control yourself and how you choose to handle them. It's your job to be able to connect them to your products and services when they are ready to make a decision.

You don't have time to lose. You need to be ready when they are ready, using the best information you have to suit the unique level of their needs.

So, create a distinct dividing line between your Hardcore and Newbie segments. Doing so will increase the opportunities for your success.

Question	Focus on Your Hardcores	Focus on Your Newbies
What do they need most?		
What can they get from you to resolve this need? What's in it for them?		
Can they easily afford your product or service? As a group, do they typically pay to have this need or problem resolved?		
Do they have money to spend?		
What's the easiest and cheapest way to reach these people with the largest expectation of return on investment?		
When you reach them, what should you say to help them make a buying decision?		

Understanding your target market and keeping your audience in mind can help you make good decisions about your goals, control your focus, organize what information to share, and choreograph your promotional tactics and sales strategies. When you have a clear understanding about the parameters of your two groups, you can find realistic answers to questions that will help build your success.

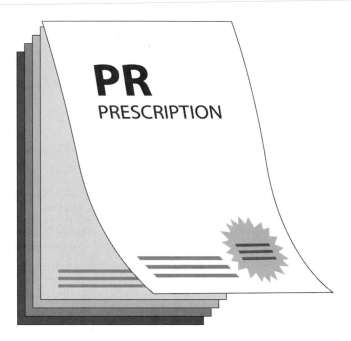

Rebecca Forster is a *USA Today* bestselling novelist, a screenwriter, and a publicity consultant (RebeccaForster.com). Are you trying to figure out how to connect with your audience and stand out? Here are some PR suggestions she offers:

- Pitch outside the box. If you're an author who plays tennis, target some tennis magazines. An artist who also teaches economics? Pitch a newspaper's education editor.
- Think kids. Mentor at the high school, share your expertise at a middle school. Kids talk to parents, parents talk to their friends, and your community relations quota goes up.
- Partner with other businesses. An author and local bookstore gather used plush toys for charity. A local dry cleaner spiffs up the toys and four newspapers cover the event.

Your "Other Guys"—the Other Niche in Your Audience

"Lately, I've been attracting customers who clearly want what I've got for reasons that I never considered promotionally important. What's going on with that?"

Back to the deck of metaphorical cards. You've thought long and hard about Hardcores and Newbies. Now, what about all those leftover cards—the third stack that includes those who are neither a Hardcore nor a Newbie?

Other Guys

When you deliberately focus your promotional attention directly on your Hardcores and Newbies, two cool things happen. The first cool thing is more Hardcores and Newbies pay attention to you. In fact, clarity and focus actually work like a magnet to attract them. The clearer you make your argument that you most definitely want them, the more magnetic you will become to them.

The second cool thing is that all the ruckus your Hardcores and Newbies cause by responding to your promotional call to action catches the attention of other prospects. Strange as it may sound, the more you proactively focus your attention on your Hardcores and Newbies, the more likely you are to also attract the interest of the third niche of your target market: your Other Guys.

Who are your Other Guys?

Your Other Guys are a whole different crowd. They are a specific group of people who have a related interest in your chosen topic—not a direct interest like your Hardcores and Newbies. Typically, these Other Guys instinctively recognize that there's something about what *you do* that is terribly important to what *they do*, even though your field and theirs are distinctly different territories.

Every target market group has its share of Other Guys—yours does, too. Your Other Guys may find more reasons to love what you do than you ever imagined. They may find unique ways to utilize exactly what you've got for purposes that surprise you.

Your Other Guys sometimes recognize things like how *their* target market connects to *your* products and services before you have a chance to see any of them as a blip on your radar screen. There are many scenarios for categories of Other Guys, but two categories stand out as potentially profitable to cultivate.

One key category is the Other Guys with unique intentions. They need your products or services for very different reasons than you ever intended.

For example, if you sell fancy spice containers to foodies, your Other Guys could be in the costume jewelry market. Somehow they've realized that your nifty spice containers are perfect for their little beads. Suddenly, you have people who want to use your spice containers to store beads, instead of spice. Presto! You're now hot in the hobby community. You don't have to change your product; you just have to expand your sales pitch.

Here's another example of how the dynamic works. If you have just written and released a book for Beatle fans, your Other Guys could be people who sell music-related stuff on eBay. You certainly didn't write your Beatle book for eBay sellers. But those eBay-ers may appreciate, say, the crash course you offer on today's generation of Beatle fans, all those fan clubs you diligently indexed, and all those special tidbits about memorabilia you carefully researched. In this case, knowing the information in your book helps the Other Guys make more money selling music memorabilia, particularly Beatle treasures.

How do you identify Other Guys with unique intentions?

- They want your products or services as-is, but for unique reasons of their own.
- Somehow, some way, you meet a need or solve a problem that you didn't know was a need or a problem...because in your corner of the world, it isn't.
- What you do is able to unexpectedly serve as some kind of cosmic extension cord that this Other Guy group needs...that is, you provide that extra thing that makes what they want to happen come to life.

What should you do about these Other Guys?

- Be aware that they exist.
- When they show up, find out who they are, what they need, and how they found you.
- Wait for them to come to you. You can't waste time dreaming up a zillion what-if possibilities that might hypothetically work for groups of Other Guys.

- Speak up if you spot an Other Guy opportunity. You don't want to ignore real opportunities when they present themselves. So, connect the dots, and see what works in real time.

Ask them the following questions:

- What makes my product or service interesting to you?
- What problem does my product or service solve for you?
- Can you afford my product or service easily?
- Is my product or service an impulse buy or something you have to save up to buy?
- What can I tell you more about so you know if you want to make a purchase?
- Where can I find more people like you?

But, how do you know if you've got a group of Other Guys that's worth your promotional outreach efforts?

Like all segments of your ideal target market, your Other Guys need to exhibit the three important qualities that should also exist with your Hardcore and Newbie niches:

- **First, each niche must be commercially viable.** You don't want to waste time or money. You want to focus your promotions on groups where there is a proven track record of needs or problems—and where there is a proven track record of people paying to resolve them.

  Their need should be big enough and bothersome enough that they will act to solve it. You need to be sure that the cost of your promotional outreach will pay off. Why pay to lay promotional train tracks to reach four people? Don't go to extreme effort unless you know it's possible and reasonable to believe you can make extreme money. Evaluate the opportunity and do the math to know what is feasible.
- **Second, the individuals in each niche must be reachable in multiples.** You really need to be able to locate and reach your Other Guy prospects as a group. You don't have time to rustle the bushes and track people down one at a time, especially if they are scattered across the landscape. You need to be able to access them through defined groups and through existing channels.
- **Third, they need to be ready for what you've got.** As we discussed in Session Three, you cannot afford to waste your efforts on maybe-never prospects. You can't afford to hang around waiting for them to eventually get ready. You need to reach the ready-right-now folks, the ones with unique needs who can be served now through your existing products or services.

The Magic of Leigh Rubin

Nobody knows the quirky humor of cows, dogs, and people better than cartoonist and sit-down comedian Leigh Rubin. His cartoon panel "Rube's" appears in more than 400 newspapers across the country. He has sold more than ten million greeting cards. An uncountable number of calendars, t-shirts, and books showcase his nearly magical humor.

Back in the days before e-mail, Leigh had regular, strict deadlines to deliver batches of twelve cartoons by snail-mail for his newspaper syndicate to process and send out to the dailies.

As one deadline approached, something magical didn't happen. Leigh only had eleven cartoons ready to send. He needed one more: one more unexpected way of looking at the world differently that would make readers laugh out loud. The clock was ticking. So, like many a creative genius under the gun, Leigh left his desk in search of inspiration and ended up in the cookie aisle at the local supermarket. That's where the magic returned. What caught Leigh's attention and his comic imagination was the cross-marketing ploy of a small sign hanging on the cookies shelves that said, "Got Milk?"

Leigh immediately visualized a cow being robbed at gunpoint and laughed. He went back home, blocked out three versions of the concept, made the deadline, and sighed with relief.

A few weeks later, when the cartoon appeared in the newspaper, Leigh realized that if the people behind the "Got Milk?" campaign could cross-market to cookie buyers, maybe he could cross market to the Milk Board. He was right. Before long, the cartoon was licensed to appear on t-shirts, in a book collection, at bus-stop benches, and on billboards—even on the side of a building in San Francisco.

PR Tip: If you see an unconventional connection between your work and the marketing efforts of others, make a contact and pursue some type of partnership.

The other key category of Other Guys is those who are looking for a stage pass into your audience.

These Other Guys don't really care so much about what your product or service is; to them, it's about the people you serve. They recognize that you have developed strong relationships with the same groups of people they want to meet.

For example, you are a pet sitter and most of your clients are affluent couples who always have a hundred questions for you about how to deal with the special needs of their four-legged friends. So, a while back you built a blog for couples who love posh pups. You've got the scoop on everything from house training dogs to traveling with dogs to making room for baby or grandbaby without upsetting the dog. All of a sudden, your blog is the hotspot for dog lovers—your clients love your warm help and so do people around the country.

When a small company and an ad agency for a large company both show up out of nowhere to pitch their separate products to you, hoping you'll write a review and share information about their dog stuff with your dog-loving community, you recognize something new and good is definitely unfolding. These Other Guys don't care if you're a pet sitter or not—they just like your audience and they want to get in front of it.

Here's another example of the same dynamic in action. You decided to sell diaper bags for new dads. The diaper bags you handle are cool looking, manly and trendy, not the usual fussy looking pink or bright blue.

To sell this stuff, you have developed a hilarious speech and even filmed a few funny YouTube clips that focus on all the funny stuff you know that new dads need to know from a guy perspective. Pretty soon you have developed a full-blown website for dads on the go that features your funny stuff and makes a great store-front for selling diaper bags online. One day you get a call from a group that wants to pay you to do your dad-on-the-go speech at some big business luncheon. They want to buy enough diaper bags to give them away to everybody in the audience. They plan to stuff the bags with coupons and brochures for baby stuff and high-end dad-type products.

How do you identify Other Guys looking for a stage pass to your audience?

- They are eyeing your audience and they make it fairly clear that you have successfully corralled a group of people that they need to reach.
- They want you to assume the role of community host because they need you to introduce them to your target market as if they are your friend or ally.
- They hang on to the way you talk and what you say because you really "get" the target audience, or perhaps you naturally convert stilted language into the appropriate lingo better than they do.
- They ask how many hits you get on your blog or your website or how big your mailing database is.

What should you do about these Other Guys?

- When these Other Guys show up, explore the opportunity carefully. Find out who they are, what they need, and how they found you.
- Be aware that they probably need you because they want you to provide them with access to the audience you've worked so hard to build.
- If you provide access to your community, get something for doing it. This might be something informal like a link on their website to yours, or an e-blast introducing you to *their* e-mail contacts, or a formal contract exchanging real money.
- Diligently guard your own reputation with your audience. Make sure there are ground rules and boundaries in place if you agree to allow your name to be leveraged with your audience to move someone else's products or services.

Ask these Other Guys some of the following questions if the situation seems relevant:

- What makes my audience, target market, or special community interesting to you?
- What opportunities do you see where we could work together?

- What kind of advertising budget do you have for promotional placement on my website?
- Would you like for me to provide focused insight on what my community would like or wouldn't like about your product or service? What kind of budget do you have that would allow me to formally review your products, services, and promotional materials?
- What kind of opportunities can you provide me?
- What kind of opportunities might exist if we did not exchange money but instead formed some kind of strategic alliance?

The key to becoming successful with your Other Guys is understanding your core target market. As you realize more about how to look at your target market, you'll notice that there's more potential for Other Guys than you ever anticipated.

Still, never lose sight of the fact that your goal is to cultivate and grow your Hardcore and Newbie base. Choreograph your promotional tactics and sales strategies to meet the needs of your Hardcores and Newbies, and you will automatically become irresistible to the Other Guys.

COACHING CLINIC #5

The Other Guys instinctively recognize that something about you or what you do is important to their own success. They are interested in a connection with you to further their own goals and meet their own needs. Build a custom profile to identify your Other Guys.

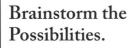

Brainstorm the Possibilities.

Have you been approached by an Other Guy?

Other Guys with Unique Intentions. They know how to utilize your products/services in a new environment.

Other Guys Looking for a Stage Pass to Your Audience. They know that your target market is a group they want to reach.

Figure out if you have an Other Guy niche. Put each Other Guy to the test by checking the appropriate box:		
Y	N	
		First, they must be commercially viable. • Are they large enough to make the promotional outreach worth it to you?
		Second, they must be reachable. • Can you locate and reach these Other Guy prospects easily? • Can you access them in large groups? • Can you access them through existing channels?
		Third, they must have an immediate need for what you do. • Are they ready now? • Will they be ready someday soon?

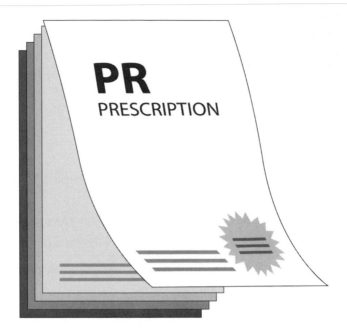

Gail F. Goodman is the CEO of Constant Contact (ConstantContact.com). She suggests:

Ask and listen. Listening is the heart of every successful relationship. People want to be heard—and to know that what they say matters to you. Establish an authentic exchange by using tools, such as online surveys, to stay in touch with customer needs. Identify "pain points" and respond with timely promotions and/ or offerings that keep people satisfied and coming back.

PHASE III

Picking and Approaching the Media

Picking and approaching the media is part science and part art. When you take the time to match your information with the right media, magic can happen. Except…when it doesn't.

On January 27, 2005, at 1:33 P.M. we received a landmark e-mail from a reporter at the *Orlando Sentinel* responding to a well-written press release about a favorite client. The reporter succinctly chose to share the following eight words: "this is the stupidest thing i've ever seen."

Well, now. That was not the magical response I'd imagined.

We printed out the e-mail and passed it back and forth across the office.

The stupidest thing he'd ever seen. Dear God Almighty. I was more than accustomed to newspapers running my press releases pretty much verbatim as story content. No one had ever responded like that. No one. Ever.

"this is the stupidest thing i've ever seen" [his capitalization].

What in the world did he mean?

"this is the stupidest thing i've ever seen" There was not much room to read between the lines. No matter how I looked at the short message, it seemed fairly clear that this guy indeed believed that the very concept we had shared was, in fact, simply stupid. Hmmm…he didn't know much about stupidity. I myself owned a collection of stupid press releases I'd received as a radio show producer, and the one I'd been sent about counting shocked trout at a fishery was hands down far more stupid than anything I'd ever written myself.

"this is the stupidest thing i've ever seen"

His e-mail was mesmerizing. In the end, we chose to feel flattered that he had taken the time to respond. It would have been easier for him to hit delete. We said to each other that it was good of him to let us hear back…magical even. We isolated his name from our database, reviewed the press release, and kept moving with it. Turns out the idea resonated with staffers at other publications better—the same concept eventually flew at the *Los Angeles Times*, *The Ladies Home Journal*, and the *New York Times*. And three years later, the very same tips became part of a successful radio campaign for the same client. I never sent that reporter at the *Orlando Sentinel* another e-mail, but if *you* do, don't feel deflated and don't you dare give up if he writes back and says, "this is the stupidest thing i've ever seen."

SESSION SIX
Raising Your PR I.Q.

"How do I actually reach my audience?"

You probably feel like yesterday wouldn't be soon enough for the kind of promotional relief you really need. But, how do you take those first steps—the right first steps—to really reach the part of the public where your customers or clients are located?

Let's start with a closer look at you.

You need to build your reputation and enhance your brand. That's where the media comes into play. You already know that the media has the power to deliver you and your message directly to thousands of prospects who might otherwise remain out of reach.

Your PR Approach Must Work for You.

You can—and must—tailor your PR approach to meet your own personal needs. It's critically important to choose promotional opportunities that are based on your skills and your circumstances so that you get the best access to the most members of your audience for your effort.

In today's rapidly changing world, there's so much excitement about New Media that it's easy to dismiss "Old" Media. It's true that the face of all media is changing by the hour, but even in this flurry of evolution, the core mission of most public relations initiatives hasn't changed and won't. PR is still about building relationships with the public and sharing your message with people who need to know about what you're doing.

In other words, so much has changed, yet so much remains the same.

On the "change" side, you absolutely need to understand what new vehicles and tools can help build relationships faster, closer, and deeper. Just don't forget, the tools are merely tools. On the "remains the same" side, you still need to do one big job—connect to your audience. No matter what old or new tools you choose to use, your goal will not waiver from the need to build an authentic relationship with your target market. You will probably want to use a mix of traditional and nontraditional tools and methods to make that happen.

Review your media tools.

So, boost your PR I.Q. and take a peek at your basic media choices for approaching publicity—traditional and nontraditional. Some tools will be more natural to you than others. Some choices will be more rewarding to you personally than others. You can pick and choose from both arenas to design a strategic plan that will work for you and your audience.

On the traditional side of the road, think Media Mode. It's not old fashioned or passé to decide to reach your audience through existing channels that are tried and true. As long as the people you want to reach are still reading magazines and newspapers and still listening to radio and watching TV, it's possible to connect effectively with them through the media they enjoy.

If that's what you want to do, you must first approach carefully chosen media targets with specifically proposed content. Your hope is that editors and producers like what you've got enough to share your message with the communities that they have built. In many cases, they have managed to corral a significant group of people you need to reach.

You may ask, "But, how do I convince the media to give me a free ride to reach their audience?" The answer is you don't. There are no free rides. If you approach the media with an attitude that screams, "Give me something free," "Make me a star," or "I want to hijack your audience for my own personal gain," well, you're going to be left standing on the side of the road. They didn't build their community for freeloaders.

Of course, you aren't a freeloader. You have relevant information that would help many members of their audience. It's your job to make sure everyone clearly understands that.

Utilizing the media takes focused effort.

Before you can approach a media contact, you must narrow down the seemingly infinite possibilities of whom to approach, what to tell them, where to find their direct contact information, and how to craft your pitch so that it can be heard above the daily noise and constant chatter of the workday world. You'll have to use methods of communication that these media leaders favor. Some will appreciate a short text on their Blackberry or a tweet through Twitter. Some would just as soon hear from you by phone, e-mail, snail mail, or the not-yet-obsolete fax machine.

But, before you get frantic about how to communicate, you first need to study print venues and broadcast venues to find the actual outlets that are the most appropriate for your message.

- **Print venues** include newsletters, newspapers, and magazines.

- **Broadcast venues** include television appearances, radio segments, and all emerging Internet content, including traditional websites, blogs, audio podcasts, book trailers, and video clips, like those you see on YouTube.

You need to consider the lead times of different media: editors and producers have production schedules that they must follow to produce their programs and publications. Consumer and trade magazines typically have a lead time of six to eight months. Newspapers, radio, and TV may have a lead time as short as a week.

Right about now you may be thinking, "Let me get this straight. I have to package the story precisely, deliver it to the perfect person in the building, at the exact right time, through their communication tool of preference, and then, in the end, release my control over what is actually said to the audience, if anything is said at all?"

Yes, that's an accurate assessment. You may nod and say, "I like the odds...I can do that."

Or, you may shake your head in disbelief and counter, "If I have to work that hard to talk someone else into creating a great piece, I would rather just do the whole thing myself and cut out the middle guy. It would certainly be faster and more productive to just do a great story than to wait on others to reject me or to tell my story in a different way than I want it told."

Using New Media

A do-it-yourself line of thinking is what motivates many people to explore the nontraditional side of the PR road. If you're thinking that doing it yourself is a good match for yourself, take a close look at all the opportunities immediately available. Some venues will help you create and showcase your information cleanly and succinctly. Some venues will provide the technical trafficking for your Hardcores and Newbies to stumble upon you or for you to access them. Some venues will help you attract and actively build your own community of followers, one real live person at a time, contact by contact.

Still, utilizing New Media effectively takes focused effort to meet your core PR goals. Before you jump into setting up accounts with popular services like Facebook, LinkedIn, Twitter, Wordpress, Typepad, YouTube and more, it helps to develop a strategic plan to utilize these wonderful tools. No one will stop you or tell you "no" if you don't have a plan. The sky is indeed the limit if you want to rant about something on a blog or launch a funny video on You Tube or sink your efforts into hosting your own Internet radio show on RadioBlogger.com.

It is all totally in your own control, and most of it will cost you nothing but time.

To get rolling, you must narrow down the seemingly infinite possibilities of how to approach your topic, what to tell your community, and how to craft your material so that your voice can be heard above the mainstream cacophony. You must also figure out how to make message distribution happen to a sizeable por-

Jay Gilbert Is Good for a Laugh

Jay Gilbert is the wickedly funny mastermind behind "Uncle Jay Explains the News," a witty, weekly video of current events created so the news of the day can, at last, be understood by innocent, ignorant, and immature minds…as well as children.

The Uncle Jay persona was invented in 1995, when a Cincinnati TV station was looking for a "soft" regular feature for its predawn newscast. Jay pitched the "Uncle Jay Explains the News" idea and got the part. It lasted about two years and won an Emmy.

Since technology now allows him to produce and present the show himself, in 2007 he decided to bring Uncle Jay back with UncleJayExplains.com.

He says he is flattered when people assume that a staff of writers and producers are behind the one-man production. According to Jay, the Uncle Jay studio is actually a "laughingly homemade setup," located in the Gilbert basement. Pole lamps do the lighting and foam mattress padding does the sound cushioning. Jay edits the video on his Mac laptop.

What extra help he gets is mostly a family affair. His thirtyish daughter is the voice on each episode's introduction, and his thirtyish son has lended his professional touch to the website's design.

In early 2009, "Uncle Jay Explains the News" started to appear on the websites of Tribune Company newspapers, as well as on some of its TV stations, increasing the possibility that the show may eventually get back onto regular TV.

PR Tip: Focus on honing your best talent and package it properly for each niche of your audience. For Jay, his talent is being funny. When not appearing as mild-mannered Uncle Jay, Gilbert is a longtime DJ on Cincinnati's WEBN. There, rock fans know him as an arrogant, snotty, and sometimes vulgar radio personality who is so funny that he has won the "Personality of the Year" Marconi Award, which is the Oscar of radio. Other audiences enjoy different sides of his sharp sense of humor. Jay has written comedy material for people as diverse as Rush Limbaugh, Air America, and National Public Radio.

tion of your potential target market because, after all, you're pretty much on your own on that part, too.

Right about now you may be thinking, "Let me get this straight. I have to package the story precisely, deliver the finished piece at exactly the right time for my audience, and also spend my own time to actually corral a likely group of prospective customers who will pay real attention?"

Yes, that's an accurate assessment.

You may nod and say, "I like the odds…I can do that."

Or, you may shake your head in astonishment and counter, "Creating new content all the time sounds like a full-time effort. When will I have time to learn how to edit my own video? Or figure out where the 'on' button is for the equipment I'll need? And most importantly, when will I have time to do what I really do—the part that is supposed to make money?"

There is a way to tailor your publicity plan to meet your own interests and needs. As you consider the different options—which are covered with more depth in the next few chapters—it will become increasingly apparent that tangible results in even one arena will indeed impact all of your efforts for success.

You don't have to do everything at once; it only seems that way. It isn't all or nothing; it just looks like it ought to be.

All promotional efforts become supportively connected in the most amazing and organic ways. A YouTube video can help a TV producer visualize a segment for a local program. A succinct blog post that shares your perspective on an important news event can land you an interview on CNN or quotes in the *Boston Globe* before you realize they'd even care about your viewpoint. A contact on LinkedIn may suddenly directly connect you to an event planner who invites you to do a keynote in Seattle. And, by following the tweets of an editor from *Newsweek*, you may find yourself being asked to contribute an essay about something you care very much about. The important thing is to believe in yourself and to be willing to do one thing to reach out to your audience—and then do another—and then another.

COACHING CLINIC #6

At this stage, mobilizing is as simple as taking three basic steps to capture the directional details you need to draft a plan that will grow as you continue to read this book.

Step One: Draft a quick wish list.

Nothing fancy, here. You just need the bare bones to establish direction.

- What types of media coverage interest you most?
- Do you dream of a particular talk show or being part of a feature story in a newspaper or on a certain news program?
- Which media do you imagine might reach your target audience best?
- Who are some key media people whom you have noticed on radio or TV, in the newspaper, or across the Internet that you like or who might like you?
- Do you like podcasts or video blogs?
- Are you interested in Twitter, or afraid to get involved?

When you're starting out, there are a hundred reasons to choose one venue over the other to acquire promotional success. But—when push comes to shove—one factor can be an important aspect that tips the scale in your favor. Ask yourself this critical question: Of all the media possibilities, what seems like the most fun?

In the long run, fun matters because it's easier for you to go the extra mile when you're having fun and it's harder for people (both media people and the people in the audience) to resist you when they sense your genuine excitement, passion, and personal interest. So, pull one option out of the media mix based on the potential for fun.

Is it radio? Is it a YouTube video?

Don't think too hard about it yet. Pick something fun for the sake of fun.

Step Two: Collect some key details for future communication tools.

Like a triage commander, it's necessary to do the best you can with the resources you have. You don't have all the facts, all the research, all the best tools—yet. Later, you'll have more resources, more information, more everything. But, right here, right now, your goal is simply to get some ideas committed to paper.

On your wish list, write out quick bites of information that you want to share. It's sometimes easier to imagine how to package your own content by considering how a producer might want to be pitched. For example, the process to create a fabulous pitch for "Good Morning America" can jumpstart your efforts to produce that idea for your own blog, or vice versa.

Answer these questions:

- What is the most relevant information to share with the media contacts you have mentioned on your wish list so far?
- What is the most interesting part about what you do that you must share?
- Why do you think each specific contact would like to hear about you?
- Are media sources covering issues that connect with what you are doing?

Make a few bulleted notes. Consider the following elements to see if your information might be newsworthy in a different way than you originally imagined:

- Do you have a major announcement or upcoming activity?
- Got new facts to share?
- Are you connected to a trendy issue?
- Any connection to current news events?
- Can you claim first, last, largest, only?

Step Three: Take action.

Things begin to shape up and get real when clear pieces start lining up. Before you can contact anybody in the media or from your prospective audience, you have to acquire some contact information, such as a mailing address, phone number, or e-mail address. Take a look at the list you have and see what it takes to track down contact information for at least three people. Start simply by considering the following:

- Who is the easiest to reach?
- Do you have any mutual friends or acquaintances?

You may realize that you only have vague general direction you'd like to pursue, like a magazine, but you don't know the name of a specific editor. Or you like a radio station, but do not know a specific producer at a specific show. These details will unfold as you continue to move through the next chapters.

Get strategic! Don't miss the best promotional opportunities of the season. Consider holidays that might have timely calendar tie-ins. Bookmarketing guru John Kremer publishes a book titled *Celebrate Today* (CelebrateToday.com), which features 18,500 special days, weeks, and months, including holidays and historical anniversaries. For example, January 17 is Pickled Peppers Day and July 24 is Amelia Earhart's birthday. With a little imagination, you can tie your PR efforts into one these dates.

- **January:** New Year's Day/New Year resolutions
- **February:** Super Bowl/Valentine's Day/President's Day/Black History Month
- **March:** St. Patrick's Day/Women's History Month/end of first quarter of the year
- **April:** Easter/Passover/spring break/taxes due
- **May:** Mother's Day/Memorial Day
- **June:** Father's Day/weddings/graduations
- **July:** Independence Day/summer reading
- **August:** Vacations/travel
- **September:** Labor Day/back-to-school
- **October:** Autumn/Halloween/beginning of last quarter of the year
- **November:** Veteran's Day/Thanksgiving/the biggest shopping day
- **December:** Christmas/Hanukah/New Year's Eve celebration

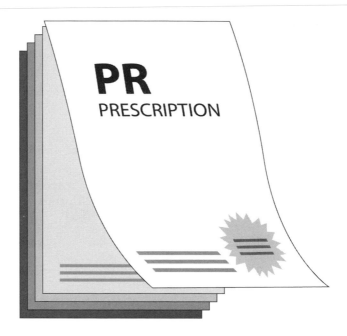

Named *Radio Ink Magazine*'s General Manager of the Year, Vicki Medina is now a marketing and advertising consultant who specializes in community relations and voice productions for national corporations. She is a pro when it comes to contacting the media:

What's the absolute best way to reach your local radio personality, television host, and newspaper reporter? Some people prefer e-mail, while others prefer a human voice on the telephone (even if it's a voice mail), and still there are those who prefer seeing a fax cross their desk. Keeping that in mind, I perform all three. Will they miss my message? No, they can't avoid me.

I also find ways to make their jobs easier. For example, I know firsthand that the media is made up of poor workaholics who never take their much-needed breaks. At my events, there's always a chance for media to grab cold beverages and a snack and they've told me they remember it and appreciate it. I also look for reasons to send a quick "thank you" whenever I can. It seems most of us are very quick to ask for things or to criticize efforts, but we often forget how important it is to recognize a media person's hard work. Every time you can make another person feel appreciated, it helps. People remember nice gestures, and being remembered is what you want in PR.

SESSION SEVEN
Think Internet

"How do I get into websites, podcasts, and blogs?"
"How do I maximize the Internet?"

The truth is, your mouse and your keyboard can help you go global. The Internet has the power and the pizzazz to promote who you are to your best audiences faster than any other media outlet can or will. People are communicating with a speed and ease that simply wasn't possible just a few years ago. Websites, blogs, podcasts, and online videos are helping transform people with passion into the heads of million-dollar companies by providing an inexpensive way out of obscurity and into the spotlight.

So, do all you can with the time and skills you have. Just do it strategically.

The first rule for Internet success is to create an Internet plan that synchronizes with your overall PR strategy and business goals.

To maximize every opportunity, start at the foundation. Use the power of the Internet to make it easy for people to spread the word about you by empowering them with the communication tools they need to get it right. You need to make it simple for everyone—especially reporters, producers, and bloggers—to instantly access your written details and acquire the photos and graphic images that they need.

Start By Creating a Media Room on Your Own Website.

If you don't have a website, you need one now. It helps to know that you can debut a website in roll-out phases. That is, you can build exactly what you need and add functionality and sophisticated features as time goes on and as your additional needs become more visible. For publicity purposes (both online and offline), the Media Room is a necessity right away—even if it is the only website page you ever build.

What belongs on your website's Media Room page?

Your core communication tools. This is the place where you formally spell out who you are and what you do. Visitors to your website's Media Room will include radio producers, TV producers, reporters, bloggers, and event coordinators, as well as, of course, members of your Hardcore, Newbie, and Other Guy audiences.

Your website's Media Room is the Internet home where you store your press kit—the digital version—in downloadable PDF files. You want to make it easy for visitors to download and print your information in a way that meets your vision of quality. For instance, package your bio in a gorgeous one-page format that's easy to print. Always offer up your foundational information in the most succinct and functional ways possible.

Digital press kits are great because of their accessibility and affordability. Cool press kits used to be expensive to design and they required lots of effort to duplicate, assemble, and distribute. Today, all that's changed. Your press materials, high-resolution photos, and graphic images can be downloadable and available in an instant if you build a Media Room on your website and furnish it properly.

Here's the checklist:

- **Personal Contact Information.** List your contact information prominently. Make sure a visitor can easily cut and paste your contact details, including your name, e-mail address, business mailing address, and business phone number. Include the URL for your site as well. Once a visitor leaves your site, he may not remember the address.
- **Bio/Personal Profile.** Present a short biography of yourself, mentioning only the details that are pertinent to your work. This should be in a printer-ready PDF format.
- **Company Profile.** If you operate as a company or other type of organization, include a PDF that succinctly outlines your company, its mission, and its history.
- **Backgrounders, Fact Sheets.** Be sure each separate sheet is clearly labeled and available in individual printer-ready PDF formats.
- **Press Releases.** Place press releases in chronological order with the most recent at the top. Again, use individual printer-ready PDF formats.
- **Awards, Reviews, Endorsements, Accolades.** These details need to be embedded in your website content so that your credentials are highly visible. But, even though the information is available throughout, don't forget to compile a list of praise in an individual printer-ready PDF format.
- **PDF Reader.** Some visitors may not have the free Adobe PDF reader, so include the following link so they may download it: get.adobe.com/reader/. You can use the Adobe PDF icon and the "Get Adobe Reader" logo on your website as the link.
- **Publicity Photos, Product Photos.** You need to have high-resolution and low-resolution images available on your website for downloading. Be sure

each image is clearly labeled. Provide multiple resolution versions of the same image. Note: 72 DPI is the lower resolution preferred by online publications and websites, and 300 DPI is the higher resolution usually required by commercial print publications. Typically, it helps if the image size is at least a 5-inch × 7-inch image for either resolution.

- **Videos.** If you have videos, make them accessible. Post clips of press conferences, product demonstrations, presentations, and more. As an alternative to placing your video on your website, post it on one of the free services such as YouTube and supply a link to the video on your website.
- **Media coverage.** Keep your media coverage alive. Include links to your TV appearances, radio appearances, as well as magazine or web articles.

Once you have a Media Room, what else should you do?

Use it. Everything you have in the way of traditional publicity materials needs to embrace and link back to your Internet connection. Don't miss the following opportunities to mention your website address:

- Business card
- E-mail signature
- Voice mail
- Fax cover sheet
- Press materials.

Beyond your website's Media Room, there are a million breaks waiting to happen online. And, while this is both exciting and true, it's also a bit paralyzing.

With so many chances and choices, it's natural to wonder, "What should I do?"

Right here is the place where you come to a fork in the Internet's super highway—a fork with multiple prongs.

Here are three ideas you need to consider:

First, it's mandatory in today's world to have an Internet presence. Currently, that Internet presence must, at a minimum, consist of an e-mail address and a website or landing page. Your Internet presence—great or small as it may be—must synchronize with your overall PR strategy to effectively impact your bottom line.

Second, although the pressure is certainly intense to be heavily online, the truth is, not everybody has the skills or the desire to write a blog, or to create videos, or podcasts. Many people do, some don't. Only you know *what* is right for you, and *when* it's right for you.

The trick is to find out, not wait around and see what happens; decide for yourself. To get rolling, you need to explore the possibilities and consider what feels right and what interests you so you can try things out, at your own speed, without being derailed from your big-picture goals by investments of time or money that don't genuinely move you closer to your objectives. In every promotional endeavor, you simply must have a positive return on investment. It's critical to your success.

Third, the basic core of PR has not fundamentally changed with the introduction of this new media anymore than it did with the invention of fax machines.

People are still people. You and your audience are still humans, no matter what tools you chose to use to build relationships and communicate with each other. That said, the development of the Internet is a lot like the development of the telephone or the invention of TV. It's here. It's part of life. It's time to incorporate Internet venues into your promotional mix. Here are four areas to explore:

- Websites
- Blogs
- Audio podcasts
- Online videos.

Websites

Your website can operate as a virtual billboard, a fully equipped storefront, or a virtual community center where everybody gathers. Too often, people who build websites forget about catering to the Hardcores and Newbies they hope will visit. So, step back and think about how you can answer the universal question that every web visitor quickly asks: "Where's what I want?"

For radio producers, TV producers, reporters, bloggers, and event coordinators, the answer will often be found at your website's Media Room. For Hardcores and Newbies, your website will likely need to effectively deliver additional informative content.

The first step to producing an effective website is to define the purpose. Ask yourself the following questions:

- What is the purpose and goal of my website?
- What do my visitors want to know?
- What are they looking for?
- What benefits can I provide?
- How do my visitors want to feel about my website?

Each page of your website should include a descriptive title, a real purpose for the visitor, and content that is truly valuable. Three things to remember:

- Each page should include a subtle call to action. That is, don't forget to tell visitors that you have products or services available.
- The text should allow as much interaction as possible. Click, click, click is good.
- All of your information must be accurate, authoritative, and up-to-date. Don't forget to update the Media Room and keep the images and content fresh.

Develop measurable objectives to help track progress and determine the success of the site. In order to know if your site is doing what you want it to do, determine how you will measure success:

- Will I rate the website's success by visitor traffic and page views, Google ratings, or some other method?
- How many website orders, say, per month, will I deem successful?
- How many contacts from the media per year, month, or week will designate success?
- What other criteria will signal success?

Clearly defined, measurable objectives will help you determine what is most important to your visitors and will help you focus your own website development efforts accordingly.

Blogs

Blogs are turning traditional PR on its head. Anyone with Internet service can become a blogger in the ten minutes it takes to sign up with a free or nearly free blogging service such as Blogger.com, WordPress.com, or TypePad.com.

Many bloggers have become powerful citizen-journalists—you can, too, if that's part of your big-picture strategy.

Don't discount the idea too quickly. It's a real possibility that blogging is the answer to your promotional issues. By the same token, don't dive in without taking a real good look at what it requires to pull off doing a blog properly.

Blogging can help you secure an active role in your field.

Through your blog, you can push key messages directly to the public. You can write your own words and use your own pictures, as well as choose your own links to other blogs, web pages, and media related to what you're talking about. Your point of view can be shared and your voice can be heard. Yet, being a successful blogger means you not only have to create relevant content, but you must also nurture your relationship with your audience on a daily—if not hourly—basis.

The idea is to keep the conversations flowing. Not just once in a while, but *all the time.* For most people, the idea of keeping up with the talk duties and chat expectations 24/7 is either exhilarating or intimidating. Either way, do a little research. Lurk around and see what exists by visiting other blogs that cater to your like-minded community.

How do you find them? Google has a blog search that will help you find the blogs that recently discussed the same topic as your topic. Check out those blogs and then check out the blog rolls of the ones you like most and go visit *their* favorite blogs. If you are excited about what you find, blogging is probably in your future, or should be.

Creating something of value for your audience should be your top objective. If you have relevant content that you want to develop and share, ask yourself the following questions:

- Do I have time to create material consistently?
- How do I feel about approaching other bloggers to link to my blog?
- How will having a blog advance my position in my field of expertise?
- Will I have to give up activities and efforts in order to carve out the time to make blogging possible?

If you offer valuable content and you make it crystal clear who you are, people will get what you're doing and genuinely understand why your stuff matters to them. *Blog on!*

Audio Podcasts

If you have something important to say out loud, start talking. All you need is a computer, a microphone, and the Internet. Podcasts can be single, individual recordings, or you can even create your own radio-style show in nearly no time and at next-to-no cost. Anyone else in the universe who has a computer can tune in and listen.

Podcasts, like blogs, are made by people who are very passionate about what they do. The big question for producing an audio podcast is: Can you produce high quality, useful content that benefits your overall promotional strategy?

Here are seven critical promotional questions you need to ask when you consider audio podcasts as part of your outreach efforts:

1. How will your product and service benefit from the popularity or mere existence of your podcast?
2. Will your podcast showcase you as an expert in your field?
3. If you decide to do a radio-style podcast, do you have the time to commit to it to give your audience sufficient opportunity to build and grow?
4. Can you access and utilize big-name guests on your podcast to leverage awareness of your own position in your field?
5. Will the information you share with your podcast audience help establish trust and awareness about you, your products, or services?
6. Will you be able to effectively use your podcast as a calling card to introduce yourself to prospective clients?
7. Will you, if you decide to, be able to infuse commercial announcements about your products or services into the podcast without jeopardizing the integrity of the podcast content?

Podcasting allows you to reach a global audience directly. Once you decide if the podcast premise is the proverbial shoe that fits your promotional plans, you can explore ways to utilize Itunes.com, get free traffic from search engines, and much more.

Online Video

Then, there's video. YouTube changed everything. Tonight, you can share an online video and be seen by dozens or even millions of online viewers before the sun rises tomorrow morning.

The idea here is to have your video go viral—make it so great that people want to pass it on just to spread the fun. Who hasn't seen the ghoulish kid tell the reporter "I love turtles," or the clip of the infamous exploding whale being blown up by the unsuspecting highway engineers who discovered what it was like to be bombed by car-crushing pounds of blubber? (If you haven't, look 'em up.)

Like blogs and podcasts, online videos can quickly take on a life of their very own. It's up to you to make sure the time spent creating online videos is worth the promotional value and that the promotional value is directly tied to increasing awareness of who you are and what you do. Or, it can be about driving viewers closer to a decision to buy your services or products. Whatever your promotional reasoning, it certainly couldn't be easier to be seen. YouTube and other video sites actually host the video files on their servers, so they take the bandwidth hit whenever the online video is viewed.

All you have to do is figure out what you want to visually share with your audiences.

Here are ten promotional ways people can effectively use online videos:

1. Commercials for your product or service.
2. Your book trailer. Promotionally, the trailer has always proved to be a winning formula for movies—now make the concept work for your book.
3. A close-up interview of yourself.
4. A how-to demonstration of your product.
5. A how-to demonstration of your service.
6. Clips from your TV, radio, or live event appearances.
7. Interviews with your happy clients.
8. One-minute tips.
9. Roundtable sessions.
10. Interviews with experts in your field

Be Transparent and Authentic.

The Internet has grown up to become one of the primary ways to build relationships directly with customers. But, relationships are still built over time by speaking in an authentic personal voice.

Here are some questions to ask yourself as you consider your possibilities:

- Do I need to create an online community or does one already exist that I can access?
- How much time do I have that I can devote to my online promotions?
- What kind of budget can I afford to spend on online promotions?
- Do I have contacts at other websites or blogs that will highlight my online efforts?
- Am I willing to personally interact with the online community?
- Am I ready for positive and negative feedback from my audience?
- Am I willing to be transparent and share personal details with my audience?
- Am I willing to create original content for online promotion?

Once you have online properties, you must promote them. Reach out to others and start a word-of-mouth campaign to get people talking about you, your website, blog, audio podcast, and/or online video. What Internet sites could use some of the information you know? Who comes up when you Google the keywords that describe what you do? Would those folks like to know more about who you are and what you do?

Remember this: Websites, blogs, podcasts, and online videos may be the easiest filter-free media to access and control, but that's what makes it even more important for you to proceed with strategy.

Sometimes the filter of mainstream media that prevents you from reaching your audience is also protecting you from reaching your audience. Sometimes going around the traditional media filter means you have the chance to make a first impression before you're really ready to make *the best* first impression.

The Internet can allow you to arrive before your time. If you were an eagle, this could be like having an audience watch you fly at that awkward stage before you've got all your feathers. You're still an eagle, of course, feathers or not, but not everyone can recognize your potential at the early stages. Your first impression might be best appreciated when you can spectacularly navigate the sky.

But, then again, being an eagle, if you focus on doing what you do and being who you are the rest will naturally work itself out. Guaranteed.

COACHING CLINIC #7

Create a media room on your own website. Make it simple for anyone—especially reporters, producers, and bloggers—to instantly access your details and acquire the photos and graphic images that they need.

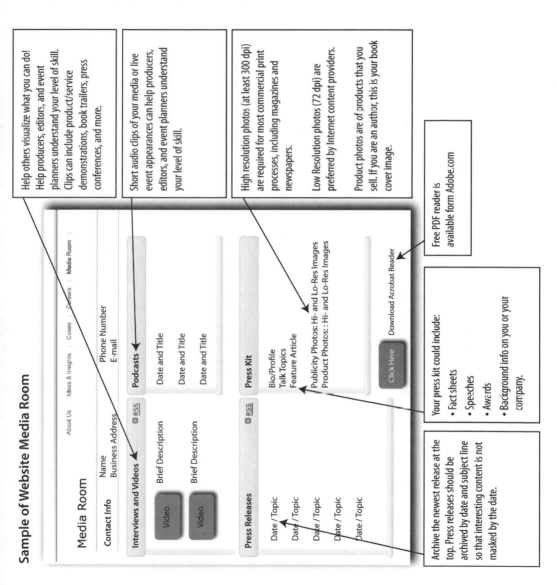

Sample of Website Media Room

Help others visualize what you can do! Help producers, editors, and event planners understand your level of skill. Clips can include product/service demonstrations, book trailers, press conferences, and more.

Short audio clips of your media or live event appearances can help producers, editors, and event planners understand your level of skill.

High resolution photos (at least 300 dpi) are required for most commercial print processes, including magazines and newspapers.

Low Resolution photos (72 dpi) are preferred by Internet content providers.

Product photos are of products that you sell. If you are an author, this is your book cover image.

Free PDF reader is available form Adobe.com

Your press kit could include:
- Fact sheets
- Speeches
- Awrds
- Background info on you or your company.

Archive the newest release at the top. Press releases should be archived by date and subject line so that interesting content is not masked by the date.

Media Room

About Us | Ideas & Insights | Cases | Careers | Media Room

Contact Info

Name
Business Address
Phone Number
E-mail

Interviews and Videos RSS

Video — Brief Description
Video — Brief Description

Podcasts

Date and Title
Date and Title
Date and Title

Press Releases RSS

Date / Topic
Date / Topic
Date / Topic
Date / Topic
Date / Topic

Press Kit

Bio/Profile
Talk Topics
Feature Article
Publicity Photos: Hi- and Lo-Res Images
Product Photos:: Hi- and Lo-Res Images

Click Here — Download Acrobat Reader

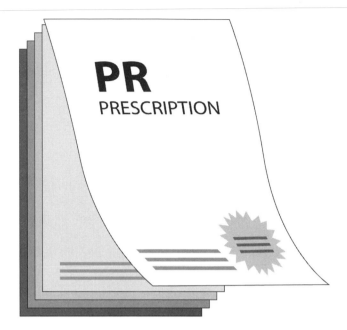

Webmaster and SEO specialist Herb Nero is a one-man IT department. His duties include SEO, search engine marketing through networks and affiliate programs, and managing the content and behind-the-scenes activities of a profitable parenting website in Hollywood. He offers the following advice:

At some point along the way, an owner of a website hears the term "SEO" for the first time and wonders "what's that all about?" Search Engine Optimization (SEO) is the art of the search as it applies to marketing on the Internet.

When you go to a search engine like Google or Yahoo! and search for a word or group of words, you get a search engine results page. The closer to the top of this page a link to your site appears, the more people will click on it.

The average search engine ranks a website based on any of over 100 criteria. It is more than technical magic, more than strong writing, more than having the right links, more than simple search engine submission—it's a combination of many of those efforts, and more, that gets you listed high up on the results page.

The best method of getting results is to build your page for the visitor and follow the guidelines recommended by the search engines. The following things matter:

- The more quality links pointing to your website, the better your website will rank.
- What other websites have to say about you matters.
- Your site's navigation setup matters.
- Using keywords help the person visiting your site (and the search engine) understand what your site is about.

From Meg Weaver, founder of WoodenHorsePub.com:

Beware of the lure of Web 2.0. Don't fall into the trap that says you have to be on the cutting edge of technology now because everybody else is—everybody else isn't. You need to feel comfortable with the technology you use; and you need to know that using "old-fashioned" communication styles may actually mean you will reach more people. The truth is, your audience may not be on Facebook or Twitter. The goal is to find the best way to reach the right people and then actually reach them. Focus on your passion and take one step at a time.

SESSION EIGHT
Think Print

"How do I get featured in newsletters, newspapers, and magazines?"

It's exciting to discover that you have more than 20,000 print publications to choose from that could be interested in who you are and what you do. It's even more exciting to realize that you only need to reach a mere handful of that number to dramatically impact your promotional efforts. One of the coolest things about print publications is how one article has staying power and is often passed around by one recipient to multiple people over long periods of time. Exposure through print can last an exceptionally long time in the marketplace and the long-term benefits can be as extraordinary as any immediate reaction.

So think "print." Your promotional choices include the thousands of consumer magazines, newspapers, trade magazines, and newsletters that are issued quarterly, monthly, and even weekly. When choosing which print publications to approach, two major factors will help you meet your goals:

1. Be sure their audience is right for you.
2. Be sure your timing is right for them.

About the Audience

Your goal is to reach as many people in your target audience as you can, people who genuinely need your products and services. By the same token, editors need your information to be a good match for them because they desperately need content that is valuable to their readers.

If *their* readership is filled with people who comprise the same group of people that make up *your* target audience, it should be easy for you to provide them with information that's focused, defined, and matches their unique editorial needs.

How do you know who their readers are? An easy way to determine the audience profile is to look at what each publication says about its readers in its advertising packages. Most print publications' advertising packages are available on their websites.

Another valuable insight is the publication's writer's guidelines. Writer's guidelines provide editorial details so freelance writers can produce the kind of articles the editors are interested in buying. These guidelines are often available on the publication's own website, and summaries of the writer's guidelines are listed in reference books like *Writers Market* or through services or websites like WritersMarket.com, WoodenHorsePub.com, MediaBistro.com, and PRtherapy.com.

Be a matchmaker. Do the necessary footwork to gather the information you need to know. When you have some viable matches, your job is to persuade the right editor at the right publication that an article featuring you or your product or service is relevant to that publication's readership. With the right spin, your information can be relevant as long as your target market overlaps with their target audience.

Good timing is critical. Even the most appropriately matched information is only useful if it arrives on time. Nobody wants to read about your tips for driving in an ice storm in the middle of August. Nobody wants to hear about must-have Valentine's Day gifts on St. Patrick's Day or Halloween. Your information is only useful if it's timely to the editors' schedules. These folks live and breathe by their internal deadlines. Each print venue has its own editorial calendar, its own production schedule that dictates when a piece will reach the audience.

If you contact the advertising department at most publications, they usually are happy to send you a copy of the publication's editorial calendar, which details the subjects to be covered in each issue.

It's important to understand that different print publications can have different schedules when it comes to what they want. You have to abide by their lead-time requirements. If you aren't giving them something that helps them meet their editorial mission, you are only wasting their time. So give them useful stuff in a timely way that's tuned in to their schedule.

How do you do that?

Get in sync. The editorial lead times of different sorts of print publications can impact and shape your promotional strategies. Decide what you want and make sure your timing is right for you and for them.

Follow These Guidelines:

Consumer magazines. These mainstream magazines consist of all those popular publications you see in the bookstores and on the grocery store racks. They are geared toward men, women, teens, or groups of the conventional public. They include *Reader's Digest, Seventeen, Good Housekeeping, GQ,* and a zillion more.

• **Lead time?** Approximately six to eight months.

• **What to pitch?** These magazines seek lively, compelling and timely information that looks like it truly belongs on the pages of their publication. Find the new spin on the same old topic. Your best shot may be to hone in on a particular department in the magazine and think of a way your topic would make that part especially intriguing. Unearth the unexpected, but realize you've got to give them something unusual and interesting that still fits in with their tone and their look.

Make your pitch brief, but detailed. Offer a calendar tie-in. A theme like Halloween or Valentine's Day is a start, but it's too broad. They need new ideas to make annual topics feel fresh and relevant. You know your stuff better than anyone else, so find a unique way to share some part of what you do—not everything, just a quick glimpse—with their readers. They want fresh ideas that are better than anything they can think of themselves.

• **Whom do you contact?** Check the magazine's masthead for the list of the editorial staff. The best person to contact is often the managing editor, associate editor, or assistant editor. Before submitting your idea, call and ask if this person is still at that position.

Trade magazines

These magazines include publications such as *Cruise Industry News, The Clergy Journal*, and *Hospitality Technology*. Readers of trade magazines are mostly the key decision makers, influencers, and upper members in the profession's field. They typically want to read about what's going on in their world. They want to know how they can do what they do better, more effectively, and more efficiently. They want the latest news, industry highlights, product reviews, upcoming events, and key stories of the latest strategic and technological innovations, industry trends, emerging technology, personality profiles, and updates.

The audience for a particular trade magazine is comprised of the people you would meet at trade shows, professional organization meetings, and technical seminars for the particular industry. Narrow in content scope, trade magazines are more technical and do contain more jargon than consumer magazines, but they strive to be every bit as understandable and entertaining for their select audience. The Hardcores from your own target market probably are readers of a trade magazine designed for your industry. If you can talk shop with the experts in your own audience, you can pitch viable content ideas to editors at the appropriate trade magazine.

• **Lead time?** Approximately six to eight months.

• **What to pitch?** Specialized information that fits the industry or a faction of it. Your best shot may be to target a department.

• **Whom do you contact?** Check the masthead. The best person to contact is often the managing editor. Again, call and check to be sure the named editor is still in that position.

Newspapers

Your choices run the range from weeklies, dailies, and alternative newspapers.

• **Lead time?** Although breaking news can be handled with very little notice, you should pitch approximately three to four weeks in advance of any set date the piece should run.

• **What to pitch?** Section-focused, newsy information that has a date and location tie-in. Consider the editor's need to make your information especially relevant to the geographic region that the newspaper covers. Whatever way the information you share can be localized, do it. Provide the editor with the direct tie-in to the readers. When you are pitching your hometown paper, mention that you are a member of the community. If you are pitching a newspaper across the country where you used to live, tell them that you used to live there and explain your connections to the region. Even if you have no personal ties to the region, focus on specific reasons this area's readers need to know the news you are sharing. A natural tie-in exists if you are involved in a local event. Decide in which section of the newspaper your story might fit best.

• **Calendar**—If you have an event, be sure the details are provided for the guide more than four weeks ahead of the event. This calendar listing tells the community what's happening locally that might be fun to attend.

• **Food**—Imaginative recipes, seasonal food stories, nutrition articles, and culinary tales.

• **Lifestyles**—Stories about interesting lives, dreams being realized, challenges being overcome.

• **Business**—Insight on trends, on-the-job news, business deals, new hires, career information, success stories.

• **Health**—From illness prevention to wellness enhancement. New scientific evidence, research, and reports on any area of health. Intelligent, informational, insightful observations explained simply.

• **Whom do you contact?** At most newspapers, the editor-in-chief is in charge of the entire paper—but, unless you personally know the editor-in-chief or you are directly referred to him or her by someone with a tight personal connection, don't go to the tip-top. Instead, go for the section editor. Names and phone numbers are usually listed on the first page of the newspaper's editorial section or deep in the newspaper's website on a contact page. If you can't find the right contact, call the newsroom and ask who the appropriate editor is for the section you want.

Newsletters

Group-focused publications may be small and the layout may smack of no-glam, but readers tend to read newsletter content carefully. Make sure your tie-in is on target for the audience.

• **Lead time?** Approximately eight weeks.

• **What to pitch?** News that specifically and directly impacts the members of the organization publishing the newsletter. One of the best opportunities for newsletter coverage occurs when you plan to appear as a speaker, workshop leader, or prominent guest at an event hosted by the organization that writes and distributes the newsletter.

But, here's the thing: It is not uncommon for newsletter editors to struggle with their organizations to get details about an event in time to promote the event. So, if you are doing an event, inquire about the organization's newsletter deadlines and graciously offer to send material to the newsletter editor directly.

Sometimes, if you are speaking at an organization's event, they will be willing to insert into their newsletter a printed flyer that you create.

• **Whom do you contact?** Check the newsletter masthead or the contact page on the organization's website to find out who your best contact is. At most of these pubs, the editor is the go-to guy or go-to gal.

What's Your Best Bet for Getting Coverage in Any Print Publication?

Be fresh, timely, credible, and accurate. Editors get hundreds of pitches a month. If you want to stand out from the crowd, know the publication and know why your story is reportable. Be a good matchmaker. Be very clear about why your information is important, interesting, and relevant to an editor's particular group of readers. Mention a specific article the publication ran recently and then explain why your product or service would be interesting to their readers.

Get good at looking ahead. To get ahead of the curve, you have to peer into the future and become futuristic and predictive with your pitches. Improve your chances for coverage by thinking far enough ahead for lead times. Start cross-referencing research on future events and be creative with your tie-ins. Think of an angle that might never occur to an overworked editor who has one foot in the future and one foot in real time all the time.

Get savvy about where your product/service could fit calendar-wise. For instance, based on affordability, problem-solving ability, usefulness, or some other reason, your product or service could be packaged to fill the annual need for a Valentine's Day story. Perhaps whatever it is that you do could be described as a great "Valentine's Day Gift for the Person Who Has It All," or a "Valentine's Gift Every Working Mom Desires," or the "Purrrfect Valentine's Gift for Cat Lovers."

By suggesting a specific angle pegged to a specific seasonal need, you're helping the journalist fine-tune a viable idea for a unique story angle that might have been missed. "Something fresh and fun that fits the market" is a whole lot better pitch than simply stating, "Here's a neat gift idea; you figure it out." Editors want new angles and fresh content. They don't want to heat up leftover information that was originally served in some other publication and they don't want to cook up every article completely from scratch.

Here are some tips to make your pitch stand out:

- Make certain the subject line of the e-mail is clear so the note gets opened.
- Send plain text e-mails—no attachments.
- Your first sentence must grab attention.
- If somebody the editor knows referred you, say it in the first two lines.
- Put your best relevant information in the first paragraph.
- Make your deepest level of understanding straightforward and crystal clear.
- Keep it brief; an e-mail should not scroll endlessly. Make it short, about a screen's length.
- Include easy-to-see headers in your e-mail that make information easy to find. Start paragraphs with headers like "About the Event," "About the Book," "About the Product."
- If you have clips of articles or of TV or radio segments, say so. Better yet, include a hyperlink in the e-mail that links to a page on the website where the clips can be reviewed.

- Add links to relevant information like a bio, press release, or images.
- Include all your contact information: address, phone and fax numbers, e-mail address, website address.

What else do they love?

- Advance leads on new products.
- Scoops about big executive changes.
- Details regarding the impacts of big news like layoffs, disasters, gas price hikes.
- Fresh bits on how to look good, be healthy, and take care of yourself.
- Unique stories starring people who've overcome hardship or had a life-changing experience.
- Tragedies, triumphs and any compelling story that has happened to a real person.
- Medical dramas.
- Interesting life stories; life lessons learned.
- Takeaway information for the readers, like tips, how-to's, and lists of resources.
- Advice on ways to help readers achieve their goals.

What do they hate?

- E-mails with attachments.
- Long rambling e-mails that go on, and on, and on…and on.
- Pitches for content that is nothing "like anything you have ever seen or heard about before" but has actually been carried in a print publication.
- The one-size-fits-all-let-me-tell-you-everything pitch.
- Follow-up e-mails and phone calls asking relentlessly, "Do you like my idea? Do you, huh?"
- Stuff that's been covered recently, unless you have a fresh angle that extends the story in a new way.

Is print worth all the effort?

Yes. No other promotional vehicle has the unique and lasting reach of print publications. Some of your very best prospects are readers of newspapers, magazines, and newsletters. The print editorial environment—as tough as it may be—actually adds credibility and legitimacy to you and your brand. In fact, print can pave the way for other media opportunities. So, if you have any print clippings, share them. They are a big part of your "wow" factor. Print is *not* a prerequisite for broadcast coverage, but sharing clippings from print publications, if you have them, can help add to your credibility and provide background details for a segment that some radio or TV producer might consider developing.

COACHING CLINIC #8

Let's focus on the print community. Start here by making a wish list of print leads, including those located in your own backyard, at important regional locations, and at the national level.

Ask yourself these questions	Brainstorm your answers	Find real contact info
1. What groups might be interested in interviewing you for their newsletter in an article that would give their members a behind-the-scenes peek at the things you do?	What groups do you belong to? What groups could you speak to at a future meeting, conference, or special event?	Name Address City, State, Zip E-mail Phone
2. Could you write an article or provide some special information, drawings, or photographs to a newsletter, newspaper, or magazine?	What can you offer?	Name Address City, State, Zip E-mail Phone
3. What newspapers exist in any of the places that you have ever lived? 4. What newspapers cover a community to which you have special family, business, or connective ties?	What are your special ties? Have you told them about your special ties?	Name Address City, State, Zip E-mail Phone
5. What magazines might be interested in a feature article about some of the cool things you do or know? 6. Which ones could quote you or run a photograph you could provide?	What makes your info relevant to them? Which ones do you love to read the most?	Name Address City, State, Zip E-mail Phone
7. What publications have run articles that made you think "wish that were me" or have made a friend or colleague say, "That should have been you"?	Why should it have been you? How can you let the editors know?	Name Address City, State, Zip E-mail Phone

Meg Weaver is the founder of WoodenHorsePub.com, an independently collected magazine database that includes contact information, editorial concepts, reader demographics, and editorial calendars for more than 2,000 magazines. She advises:

- Don't spray your message out to the world to anyone and everyone who might possibly be remotely interested. PR spam can hurt you.
- Know the difference between consumer magazines and trade magazines. Consumer magazines consistently need something that promises readers ways to do things better, from cooking tips to ways to exercise. Trade magazines are professional publications that need more in-depth, factual information that can be used on-the-job.
- Targeting the right people and understanding what they really need is more important today than ever before.

SESSION NINE
Think Broadcast

"How do I break into radio and TV?"

If you're a celebrity or a world-renowned business guru, you might expect invitations to come pouring in from shows like *Good Morning America* or *The Early Show* or even XM Radio's *Oprah and Friends.*

But, what if you aren't quite so popular…yet?

Unless your market is restricted to a small geographical area, national programs should still be on your list of targets. In fact, radio and TV are almost always an important part of good overall media strategy. So, set your sights and start moving.

The first step? Start with what's most easily within reach.

Go Local.

Local program producers can be as easy to reach as your own telephone or your own car. Local morning shows provide many opportunities for you to get screen and air time. And "local" doesn't necessarily mean your own backyard. Virtually every city has its own morning news show on the local TV affiliate of Fox, NBC, ABC, and CBS, and virtually every city has its own wacky, zany, or beloved radio drive-time crews, too.

Get out there and connect with the broadcast media that best reaches your audience—it's worth it. For TV, you have to be at the studio, so plan your pitches to synchronize with your willingness to make travel plans. For radio, you can be a guest from the comfort of your own home, while wearing your pajamas if you like. The big deal here is: Don't underestimate the value of the local segment.

If local to you means that your local programs are in New York City or Los Angeles because that's where you live, think of ways to go local in a less competitive market. Visit a friend in Cincinnati, or Helena, or Dayton, or Kansas City, where coverage is not so competitive and where coverage might be even more likely *because* you're visiting.

Take advantage of the options that work best for your needs. Since local programs exist in every geographic area across the country, you have a chance to reach significant segments of your target market in cities, counties, and whole states, one at a time.

For instance, if you have an aerospace-themed novel, locate aerospace communities that exist around military bases and pitch their local stations. If you have a product that is the answer to teaching older adults to use the computer, pick media in locations that have huge retirement populations.

If you are an expert in baby whispering or horse whispering, track down local media in top communities with the largest populations of new parents or equine lovers. Think about where the people in your market live and plug yourself into their media.

You can use local coverage to transform your national image. Each time you appear on a local show, you gain valuable experience and you should come away with a clip of your interview. Get enough of these local audio and video clips and you can create a collage that showcases your interviews. Remember that seeing is believing. It's important to make access to your video clips easy for media contacts to view. You can offer the clips as a polished collage on a DVD or provide links to video files from your website. The barriers between you and national audiences will magically disappear when you make it easy for national producers to understand that you can deliver interviews at the quality required for their national productions.

What do you have to do to wake up local morning shows?

Contact the right person. For radio, the program director, the producer, or the news director are good contacts to get things rolling. At some radio stations, the on-air hosts themselves may be producing the work. For TV, the segment producer, news director, and program director are titles of the people you want to contact. If you spot a likely TV or radio personality, call the station and ask for the name and contact information of the producer for the program featuring that personality. The assignment desk is another likely place to start.

Get off on the right foot by researching the shows you pick to pitch. Before you contact producers, go onto the station's website and check out its top stories. Get a sense of what's happening in each particular city. Keep in mind the personality and spirit of a particular community and realize that programs on affiliate stations can differ widely from each other and from those of their national parent.

What flies in New York might not fly so well in Kansas City or Salt Lake City or Lansing. Each community's viewers have different cultural sensibilities. Do what you can to showcase the part of your story that is most appealing to the locale. You have to be ultra-relevant for the locals.

Send them information that immediately gets their attention. The most important thing you need to do is keep your pitch local—micro-local. Local events that are free to the community are good news pegs. Ties to local charities and nonprofits are interesting. Name-dropping connections to local celebrities, socialites, hometown heroes, or political leaders usually get noticed. In any form of pitch—e-mail, telephone, or snail mail—you must cover the following elements:

- Very briefly cover who, what, where, when, and why.
- Lead with the most compelling information.
- Provide local relevance.
- Offer to send additional information.
- Ask for what you want. If you want to be a guest, say so.

Time your approach carefully. On any deadline-filled day, nobody wants to be interrupted unless it is with a breaking news story that's better than the one they are already working on. Here are some guidelines to follow:

- **Radio: Generally call between 7:30 A.M. and 8:30 A.M. or after 10 A.M.** Steer clear of radio stations at the top of the hour when the hourly news broadcast may be their only focus. Avoid calling right before or during the show, newscast, or drive-time segment that you are trying to pitch.
- **TV: Generally call between 10 A.M. and 11 A.M. or 1 P.M. and 3 P.M.** Avoid calling right before or during the show or newscast segment that you are trying to pitch.

Keep the pitch straightforward. Here's a phone script for you to follow when you call:

- This is who I am.
- This is what I'm doing that will interest you and your audience.
- This is why I think you should know this right now.

If you get voice mail, deliver an even quicker pitch, slowly reciting your phone number at the beginning and the end of the message. Here is a voice mail script for you to follow:

- This is who I am.
- This is my phone number.
- This is what I'm doing that will interest you and your audience.
- This is why I think you should know this right now.
- This is my phone number.

Saying the phone number twice gives them two chances to write it down, two chances to hear the number if a digit sounds confusing, and a chance to hit replay to catch it again at the front of the message without having to listen to the whole message.

Expect six possible responses to your initial contact. Here's what they may say and what you need to do next:

1. **No response to your e-mail, voice mail, or snail mail.** So much silence you can hear the crickets in the distance. This is the most common and the most maddening response. Your natural impulse is to cover your bases and call every single person who works in the building. But, if you do, your persistence will be deemed irritating. People at the same station, especially on the local level, talk to each other. They even share the same coffeepot and sometimes sit together in the same overcrowded little room. You want to get as much coverage as possible, but you don't want to be labeled as the winner of the "biggest pain in the butt" award for harassing the whole lot of them.

2. **"No. I'm not interested."** Even though you'd rather respond by saying, "Not interested in my life's work? Why the heck not, you big dunderhead?," thank them instead. Always remember that nobody owes you the time of day. Any response at all is better than silence and "No" often means "Not now...not yet...maybe some other time."

3. **"I need more information."** Most will request relevant information by e-mail, mail, or fax. You may worry about the need for a big, fancy press kit to exude a certain sort of importance and style. Big fancy press kit or not, when it comes to getting the message across, what they really need is the message broken down into its simplest form. They have to know exactly what they are really dealing with. Focus your energy on substance and clarity, and provide the exact information they requested. Nobody will miss the fancy schmancy press kit part.

4. **"Send me one."** Send whatever it is that you have mentioned for review. Maybe you have a new book, a video, a sample product, or a press kit. Don't make producers wait. The cover letter could be a brief memo that gets straight to the point: "Thank you for discussing _____ with me. At your request, I have enclosed _____. I will follow-up with you shortly. If you have any questions, contact me at...." Make sure the basic information is in the package with your contact information. Follow up the day the material is scheduled to arrive.

5. **"Not for me, but I'll share this with somebody else here who might be interested."** This is a good sign. Let them pass you around to each other, but try to keep up with the play-by-play of the passes. Ask if you can have the direct contact information to follow up with the referral contact.

6. **"Are you available?"** Yes, you are. Set up the interview.

Dealing with radio and TV can be remarkably similar because they are both broadcast venues. But they are also terrifically different. In fact, the two venues typically help you meet different promotional goals and they require you to develop and utilize different sorts of skill sets. Here are some differences you should know about:

Radio

For most people, radio can be a better place than TV to get started for several reasons. The major benefit of radio is that you have more control over the content than you do on TV. Radio interviews allow you to casually mention your contact information and even the buying details for your product or service without ever sounding like a sales person in the process.

Early on, radio can be easier to break into than TV. Mainly, you don't actually have to be in-studio to do a cool segment, so doing radio is simply easier logistically for everyone. But radio is also easier on a development level, too. By nature of appearing on radio programs you will naturally develop the additional skills you need to transition to TV comfortably.

Why?

On radio, you can pay attention to the quality of your content without worrying about how you look. It's not that radio doesn't require you to be polished; radio producers and hosts definitely demand high quality. But it's easier for you to come across as polished when you don't have to worry if viewers can see the nervous tic in your eye, if your hair looks good, or if the camera was on close-up for that split-second of horror that crossed your face when you couldn't immediately recall the name of your own company or your own phone number.

The more radio you do, the better you become at speaking comfortably, confidently, quickly. You get better because you have a chance to focus on building your talk repertoire. Yet, radio is not a dress rehearsal or a start-up strategy.

Radio offers access to some of the most finely-tuned niche markets imaginable. Generally speaking, your goal on radio is to be a guest on a specific radio program or to do a segment during morning drive-time or afternoon drive-time when much of the audience is going to work or coming home from work and is listening to the radio in their cars.

Although ratings vary from station to station, the weekday afternoon drive usually doesn't have as large an audience as the morning drive, but it often catches consumers when they are in a position to make a purchase decision, like swinging by a store to check out a product they just heard about it.

Here's what you want: Specific radio programs or the morning and afternoon drive-time shows typically have room to feature you in segments, interviews, or in conversational banter with on-air personalities.

You could pitch yourself to do relevant segments that entertain or inform audiences. Based on the station format, the tone of these conversations and the focus of the subject matter could range from family-friendly to raunchy to spiritual to all-business. The format of the radio station defines who you'll find in the audience. To be a viable guest candidate, deliver what is most relevant for listeners.

Get in sync. The lead time for most radio segments is very short. Decide what you want. Alert them to the possibilities three weeks ahead of time and keep in close touch the week before.

Focus on the audience. Your big goal is to reach *your* target market. You need the station's audience to be a good match for you—comprised of people who genuinely need your products and services. Yet, when you pitch yourself, your focus needs to be on fitting seamlessly into the station format. Spell out the connection between the show and what you offer; explain why this connection will be of interest to their listeners..

What radio format is the right fit for you? The one that is listened to by the biggest share of your target market. Below are some of the station formats that exist in communities across the country. Start by looking at the station formats, study the differences between them so you can eliminate the obvious no-goes, and then focus on seeking opportunities with the ones that seem to fit.

• **Adult Contemporary (AC)** and **Hot Adult Contemporary (HOT AC).** Stations with these formats typically describe themselves as "Today's hits, yesterday's classics" or "Classic hits of the 70s, 80s, and 90s, plus a blend of the best new songs." Hot AC is practically the same as AC only slightly livelier, with hotter choices of soft rock music. The DJ's tone is typically family-friendly.

Dayna Steele, Entrepreneur Extraordinaire

It all started with a dare in college. A local radio personality challenged a group of friends to audition for the new university radio station. Dayna Steele took the challenge, hoping to get a date with the deejay. She never got that date, but she went on to become one of the top female radio personalities in the country.

"I didn't play 'Stairway to Heaven' any better than any other deejay," says Dayna. "What I did do was work harder, work smarter, network with everyone, and take advantage of every bit of free publicity I could."

She didn't stop at spinning discs; she went on to excel in talk radio, being included in *Talkers Magazine*'s "100 Most Important Talk Show Hosts."

This enterprising entertainer eventually moved on to become an entrepreneur, creating TheSpaceStore.com. She also created Smart Girls Rock (SmartGirlsRock.com), a product line to encourage girls to "make smart the new cool." This idea came from her experience watching customers at The Space Store decline to buy science experiments, flight suits, and space toys for girls. "I just couldn't believe parents would balk at buying any of the space stuff for their daughters, especially at a time when the first woman was getting ready to command a space shuttle mission."

So, Dayna returned to her rock background long enough to write *Rock to the Top: What I Learned about Success from the World's Greatest Rock Stars*, a business book based on lessons she learned from rock stars such as The Rolling Stones, Van Halen, and Def Leppard.

Dayna took a serendipitous event, mixed it with hard work, intense networking, and an affinity for publicity and built a successful career. In 2008, she was named one of the "35 People Who Inspire Us" by *Readers Digest Magazine*.

PR Tip: Never underestimate the power of intensive networking and free publicity. These will open doors you never imagined.

• **Oldies.** This format is meant to take you back to yesteryear by playing rock 'n' roll music released during the 1950s, 1960s, and 1970s. These stations sometimes recreate the sound of old AM stations and may even do TV trivia. Sample artists: the Beatles, Aretha Franklin, Elton John, the Beach Boys. The tone is usually good-humored and nostalgic.

• **Classic Rock and Rock.** Classic rock stations play a limited amount of current releases, along with music released during the 60s, 70s, and 80s. Sample artists: AC/DC, Pink Floyd, Led Zeppelin, Jimi Hendrix, and the Rolling Stones. Rock stations play newer stuff with sample artists like Metallica and Godsmack. The tone is usually edgy, with dark to raunchy humor.

• **Smooth Jazz.** Classic hits and new, emerging artists in the contemporary jazz and pop fields. Easy-going popular music designed to set a mood with a jazzy, medium-tempo or hip-hop beat along with a blend of contemporary instrumental jazz and smooth vocals is the fare here. Sample artists include Kenny G and Sade.

• **Jazz.** Vocals or instrumentals ranging from Dixieland and blues-influenced ballads of the 1930s and 1940s to the sophisticated sounds of the current era. Sample artists: Nat King Cole, Billie Holiday, and John Coltrane.

• **Blues/R&B.** Here you'll find a mixture of hip-shaking soul music, old- and new-school jazz, industrial-strength rhythm and blues, classic rhythm and blues, Motown, classic soul, and classic top-40 songs from the 60s, 70s, and 80s.

• **Alternative.** Radio with a spine. Music that matters. These stations support local music and may play the best homegrown bands. They focus on experimental and contemporary music.

• **College.** Student-run radio that offers a variety of music genres, news, information, public affairs, and instructional programs. These stations often mix many styles of music right next to each other. You may find classical music and fine arts programming mixed in with cutting-edge alternative music, blocks of jazz, blues, new age, urban, hip-hop, Latin, and top-40 oldies.

• **Urban/Hip-Hop.** New and classic hip-hop, rap, R&B, and soul. Many urban stations focus their appeal to adults rather than teenagers. Sometimes characterized as "Urban AC," they may include soul and R&B hits dating back twenty years or longer. Sample artists include: 50 Cent, Nelly, Mary J. Blige, and Snoop Dogg.

• **Country Music.** Wide-ranging treatments of country music exist. These formats may blend classic country, Western, bluegrass, and alternative country. You may hear heartfelt ballads, songs with Southern, traditional, or rural American influence. The tone is typically upbeat and family-friendly enough for any parent with a minivan full of kids.

• **Business News.** Radio that makes you money. This is business and financial information combined with the latest local and national news and analysis. Your chance to hear talk about what is going on behind-the-scenes.

• **News.** The news format offers continuous local, national, and world news twenty-four hours a day. Expect the latest news, traffic, and weather from across the street or across the world.

• **Talk.** Hot talk about pop culture, politics, entertainment, and comedy is dished up here. Compelling talk on health, wellness, fitness, and medicine is often part of this format. Look for specific programs to find the best fit for your information.

• **News Talk.** "We're taking your calls." This format offers news, interviews, and analysis of major events that cover a wide variety of live and local content, along with dynamic national talk show personalities.

• **Public.** NPR offers news, music ranging over a wide spectrum including jazz, blues, reggae, international, country, cabaret, and more. Here you'll find programs that inform and educate the listeners on topics that will help them lead happier, healthier lives.

• **Sports.** Commentary by experts and phone call participation by listeners, dealing with all types of sports is the meat of this format. They may air play-by-play sports broadcasts, breaking news, expert reactions and analysis, game previews, features, news briefs, challenging trivia, and lively phone rants.

• **Religious.** Stations may vary widely in this category. You may hear music, chants, prayers, interviews, lectures, recorded radio feeds, sermons, readings, prayers, and independent music that may range from Christian rock to religious instrumental to Southern gospel and beyond.

• **Gospel.** Presented with a stream of gospel tunes and sermons, listeners are promised exposure to life-changing messages. Play list includes Christian, hip-hop, traditional, urban contemporary, and others.

• **Christian Contemporary or Christian Rock.** Characterized as music with hope, this variety of music ranges from contemporary praise and worship to Christian rock and heavy metal to Christian alternative music. Stations typically have teaching segments, news, music information, local concerts, and special events.

Television

Meanwhile TV, and local TV in particular, is a totally different opportunity to build a wonderful relationship with your target market. Local TV offers great regional exposure, but the bar can be high even at the local level.

You have to think visually about every segment you pitch. Understanding what the components of a segment are will help you imagine better ways to craft the segment ideas you are pitching.

If you watch any newscast—regional or national—you will see that you've got two components for most segments: the talking head and the b-roll.

• **The Talking Head.** A "Talking Head" is an in-studio guy or gal talking to the viewers directly through the camera. But, a Talking Head who talks too long is boring for viewers. So, sometimes the Talking Head talks to the Other Talking Head. The Other Talking Head can be a cohost, or an in-the-field reporter, or an eyewitness at the scene, or it could be you. If you are the Other Talking Head, you are probably a guest in studio, or a guest out at an event, or the expert weighing in on matters at hand through a quick sound bite. Visually, ping-ponging between the Talking Head and the Other Talking Head is more interesting to watch than looking at one Talking Head talking alone. But even two Talking Heads can become boring to watch. That's where the b-roll comes in.

    • **The b-roll.** These are the cutaway video shots that allow viewers to see something besides Talking Heads. The b-roll helps illustrate what the Talking Heads are talking about. For example, while the Talking Heads are talking about implementing new education techniques, the b-roll may be showing a classroom of kindergarten kids sitting in a circle learning something. Or, when the Talking Heads are talking about preserving your valuables in case of a weather-related disaster, footage of last week's tornado tearing up a row of houses may screen. The b-roll may establish the location, setting, essence, age group or some kind of illustratable point. Stations have budgetary constraints, so b-rolls aren't major movie productions. Many television stations have tape libraries with stock footage that they can use to illustrate a particular segment, kind of like stock clip art you might use to illustrate a flyer.

Many TV crews will go to a location if they know there's something fresh and interesting to capture on video besides more Talking Heads at tables or behind podiums. If you have something to share, help them visualize the scene. Tell them about the opportunity to capture shots of the mother hippo arriving at the zoo, the chance to video the world's longest sandwich being built, the opportunity to film a group of young volunteers cleaning up the neighborhood, the parade of 150 kids bringing storybook characters to life at the local bookstore bash.

Make local TV appearances part of your travel plans. Opportunities to appear exist in the daily morning shows, but may also be available on midday, evening, and nightly broadcasts of the local news. Local events that are free to the community, ties to local charities and nonprofits, interactions with local celebrities, hometown heroes, and political leaders are often newsy enough for coverage. Remember, the placements you secure at the local affiliate level can be leveraged to give you entrée to the nationals.

If you are going to collect video clips to build a collage of appearances you've made, follow these tips:

    • Remember that seeing is believing. It's important to make access to your video clips easy for media contacts to view. You can offer the clips as a polished collage on a DVD or provide links to video files from your website. The barriers between you and national audiences will magically disappear when you make it easy for national producers to understand that you can deliver interviews at the quality required for their national productions.

• Consider a variety of ways to share your message so that your appearances don't feel repetitive or scripted.

Get in sync. Like radio, the lead time for most TV segments is very short. Decide what you want. Start alerting them to the possibilities three weeks ahead of time and keep in close touch the week before. Realize that small stations that only have one evening newscast typically need to tape events between 10 A.M. and 4 P.M., so that they have time to edit the tape and prep for the evening newscast.

About the audience. Since your aim is to reach *your* target market in *their* geographic community, make your piece particularly relevant to the local crowd.

- Do understand the cultural influences of a particular region. What's perfectly acceptable in San Francisco may simply shock Oklahoma City.
- Do deliver a segment that's valuable to viewers.
- Don't pitch a story that doesn't have a local tie-in.
- Do pitch "visualize-this" ideas if the segment lends itself readily to more than the in-studio Talking Heads.
- Do respond to producers quickly and help them out on a deadline.
- For national pitches, realize that most national producers are surviving under tremendous time crunches. More often than not, they work from Blackberrys. Make sure your e-mails are succinct and without attachments.

COACHING CLINIC #9

Let's focus on the broadcast community. Start by making a wish list of radio and TV leads, including those located in your own backyard, at important regional locations, and at the national level.

Ask yourself these questions	Brainstorm your opportunities	Find real contact info
Local/Regional Radio: • Do you listen to any radio shows where you might be a good guest? • Do you have friends or acquaintances who work in radio? • Could anything you do enhance a segment or program on a radio station you like? • Are you involved in any activities that radio personalities should know more about?	Why would you be a good guest? How will you get the producer's attention?	Name Address City, State, Zip E-mail Phone
National Radio: • What national programs do you listen to now?	What relevant information could you supply to the producers?	Name Address City, State, Zip E-mail Phone
Local/Regional TV: • How can your idea for a segment be strong visually for these affiliates of ABC, NBC, CBS, Fox, or special cable channels?	Do you have travel plans? Do you have events planned that would interest local TV?	Name Address City, State, Zip E-mail Phone
National TV: • Again, how can your idea be strongly visual for *Oprah*, *Good Morning America*, *The Early Show*, *Ellen*, *The Today Show*, or other national shows?	Do you watch any TV shows that seem like a perfect match where you might be a good guest?	Name Address City, State, Zip E-mail Phone

Here are some more tips from radio and TV coach Dan O'Day:

- **About your introduction:** Provide the host with an introduction that is brief enough for him or her to sound conversational while making you sound like the biggest expert in your field. Instead of, "Mary Smith is president of Mary Smith Enterprises, a multi-discipline consulting firm that specializes in banking, finance, loan origination, public relations, strategy, and HR issues including hiring, firing, and ongoing employee improvement metrics, say something like: "Mary Smith is one of the world's leading experts on career enhancement. Her latest book is entitled *Your Corporate Parachute.*"

- **About sound bites:** Sounding overly rehearsed is not the result of knowing your material too well or of too much rehearsal. It's the result of not investing your words with the freshness and intensity you gave them when first you spoke them. With interviews, you'll be asked the same questions repeatedly (especially, of course, if you provide the lead questions to the interviewer). If you're a pro, you'll know exactly what your answer is going to be—but you'll make it sound as though no one has ever asked you that question before; it will appear to be a smart, challenging question which you're thoughtfully answering for the first time.

SESSION TEN
Think Live Events

"Are live events important?"
"What if I hate microphones and big crowds?"
"What if I dream of becoming a speaker on the professional speaking circuit?"

Speaking? In front of people?
    When you hear "speaker" or "live event" you may instantly envision standing behind a podium trying to imagine a crowd of strangers in their underwear. That's right. A podium. A group of strangers. Way too much underwear. No wonder the thought of becoming a speaker of any proportions slips to the bottom of the promotional list for most PR seekers.

The good news is live events really don't have to be that way at all.

Sharing your message person-to-person is an important part of every promotional strategy. But, if you *don't* like podiums, don't worry. You can successfully participate in an endless supply of live events without ever lecturing onstage and without ever trying to picture members of the audience in their boxers, briefs, thongs, and panties. And, if you *do* like podiums, your talent to talk to your audience will help catapult you toward success.

When you believe in what you're doing, you absolutely must do what it takes to reach the people who need your products and services. Interacting with your target market face-to-face can earn you the street credentials you need and can reward you with the insight you need to communicate with them effectively. At every stage of the journey—from a first-time presentation to a few people around a table to a seasoned speaker's placement—live events should be and can be tremendously fun and rewarding.

Here's How to Do It.

Focus on what you love the most about what you do and let your passion guide the way. If you set your sights on sharing what you love with people who you genuinely believe should hear about what you know and do, you'll get where you need to be. If you refuse to waver from the goal to reach your target market, the how-to-do-it details will fall into place no matter what your level of speaking experience or comfort.

The key is keeping your passion intact and your eye on reaching the audience with information that connects loosely or tightly to your products and services. When it comes to being a good speaker, choose the topics and tones that work for you, what feels right, and what personally fits.

As you seek opportunities, realize that live events can range from simple to extravagant, casual to very la-ti-dah, dry to rowdy. You know the difference between what makes your skin crawl and what feels exhilarating. It's up to you to actively seek and choose audiences and activities that align with your personality and your comfort range. Choose opportunities that help enhance who you are and what you do, as well as help bring promotional exposure to your products or services. Don't be afraid to stretch and grow into territories that are a natural extension of where you are now.

It is absolutely possible to find live events that are genuinely right for your unique personality and a perfect fit for your ever-growing skills as a communicator. Take time to explore the wide array of possibilities. Would any of the following opportunities match your interests:

- appearing as a special guest at a group gathering
- instructing a class or a series of classes
- demonstrating a skill
- performing a how-to demonstration
- training a group of volunteers
- teaching a seminar or leading a workshop
- appearing as the guest speaker at a company's lunch-and-learn session
- leading a breakout session at a conference
- participating as an expert on a special panel at a convention
- moderating a roundtable discussion
- serving as the keynote speaker at a symposium
- reading a selection of your book at an author event
- fielding a formal Q & A session at a school assembly or club meeting
- managing a table or booth at a free community event
- meeting with influencers or decision makers one-on-one
- leading an interactive, hands-on activity
- teaching a local college extension course?

Be proactive. Consider where you want to be and what you want to do. Design your promotional strategy to help you get exactly the kind of speaking gigs you want. Connect the dots between A) the topics you can talk about easily and B) the ways you can naturally bring some awareness of the fact that your products or services exist. The goal, of course, is not to be a live walking, talking infomercial spouting out prices or sales features. You are not trying to use your speaking opportunity as a direct sales presentation. The goal is to connect with the audience, win their attention and trust, and make sure they like you enough to ask for more information.

Think the entire process through carefully. Identify viable live event opportunities that exist within your segment of the marketplace and make contact with the decision makers who manage venues that interest you. Then, request details about their needs and how they make their decisions. Find out about the kind of time frames, deadlines, expectations, and requirements that are part of the process.

You have to begin somewhere, so start where you are. From the small town to the big city, every community has worthwhile opportunities—some even exist in your own backyard. Make preliminary efforts to reach out to the people who are within your reach. How do you get things rolling?

- **Consider local groups.** Do you or your circle of friends know about any groups or clubs that might be interested in having you speak briefly to their membership? Ask your friends, family, and anyone who you see on a regular basis for their ideas and their referrals. On any given day, you can find a Rotary meeting, a book club, a church group, a community center, an educational class, or a special-interest organization that meets regularly. Any of these folks might enjoy your guest appearance if they simply understood the connection between you and them.

  When a lead presents itself, follow up. Call the club president, program coordinator, or group leader. Say, "I am interested in talking to you about speaking to your group. I need some information about the opportunities you may have for speakers, such as what your group is most interested in. What do they need?"

- **Think educationally.** Are there any local classes that might benefit from your visit? Ask the class instructor, "Do you need a guest to share information about my specific topic as part of one of your class sessions?"

- **Consider the nonprofit community.** Volunteer to help a nonprofit group with a mission that overlaps into your field of interest. Do a training session for their volunteers. Be the dinner speaker at an awards ceremony. Or offer to conduct a stand-alone event held as a fund-raiser. This can work as two-way benefit. Live events naturally attract media attention since they make interesting feature stories. Media exposure is as important to a nonprofit as it is to you. Figure out how your expertise enhances what the nonprofit does in the community or how it could help illustrate the importance of what they do. Then address this opportunity by suggesting such an event to the nonprofit's event coordinator.

- **Offer your own workshop at a school, at a library, or business.** Ask, "Would your group like me to share my expertise with you at a future meeting or at a special event?" Be ready with a short proposal of what you would cover and how it might benefit the organization's audience.

- **Think local and beyond.** Live event opportunities exist at local, regional, and national levels. Strategically, key local events can be every bit as valuable as regional or national ones. Local events often are not as competitive or as sophisticated as events at the other levels and so they may be easier to line up and present at.

Are there any regional or national conferences that you could participate in? *Do your homework.* A group may make a formal call for proposals, accepting suggestions and submissions for program speakers. A call for proposals is often posted on the group's website and applications are usually requested four to twelve months in advance of the planned event.

Speakers who submit proposals are typically evaluated on a series of selection criteria like relevance to the planned program, expertise in the field or topic, speaking experience, and availability. If a call for proposals is not listed on a particular website, contact the conference coordinator and ask, "What do you need in the way of speakers for break-out modules, panels, or keynotes?"

Taking the Next Step

As your brainstorming begins to produce a list of real possibilities, several thoughts should present themselves. You'll probably wonder:

- What kind of information will event coordinators want?

- What will it take to meet their expectations?

- What kind of material should be ready for follow-up after initial contact is made?

In other words, once you open this can of worms, what do you need to do next? After you have identified some prospects and opportunities, you must organize and articulate your ideas in a format that makes it clear to the person you have contacted why he or she should invite you to make the presentation.

It helps if you approach every situation knowing what *you* want. That's not to say that you should bulldoze your way in and make crazy demands. You need to listen to people, consider what others want, and remain open to compromises and concessions. But, first and foremost, know what your goal is and what you are comfortable with. Decide what sort of speaking format you're willing to perform in, what sort of format you need to avoid, and what you are looking to achieve by participating.

Package your content. Speakers are expected to present engaging as well as informative program content. Package your information so others can understand how the audience will benefit from your presentation. Spell it out. Clear subject titles and content descriptions with specific information tend to generate the most interest. Share the following information about each topic you propose:

- **What is the title?** Clever is great, but clarity is essential.
- **What is the subject matter?** Provide a straightforward description of your session in about fifty to seventy-five words.
- **Characterize your intentions.** Use one or two signpost statements to help clarify your presentation goals. You might say something like, "This ninety-minute presentation is designed to develop the knowledge, skills, and cultural acumen necessary to conduct business in today's Japan." Or you might characterize the goals like this: "This hilarious lunch-and-learn presentation includes in-the-field stories that will both entertain and offer important how-to tips."
- **Use bullet points.** List a few take-aways for the audience as bulleted statements. These short sentences should note distinct pieces of knowledge that you expect attendees will "take away" as a result of time spent with you.
- **Mention handouts.** If you will have handouts, say so. Handouts are often valuable to attendees and important promotionally. They can be as simple as a list of suggested resources or a page of how-to tips.
- **Say who you are.** Early on, event hosts will need biographical information about you to decide if they want to book you. Later on, they will need to share that biographical information about who you are and what you do with attendees. Provide a short biography or profile of yourself—about fifty to 100 words in length. Your bio needs to sound matter-of-fact, clear, and concise. It should connect the dots by characterizing your experience or accomplishments that are most relevant to your presentation. Bios are usually written in the third person, like you are talking about someone else.

Don't lose focus. As specific speaking options materialize and unfold, it may become necessary for you to understand and meet the needs of many diverse venues. The problem with this is that as you focus on meeting *their* needs, you may lose sight of *your own* needs and *your own audience's* needs. The excitement of being wanted by many different organizations may tempt you to drift off your own promotional course and even lose sight of your own mission.

Determine which events are good matches for your promotional goals. Make some decisions about how you can meet your PR goals efficiently and effectively using these events. The bottom line is you only have so many hours in the day. Lassoing and preparing for an event takes a lot of time and energy and there's no guarantee your effort will pay off promotionally. Clearly, a primary goal is to strategically choose live events that match your promotional needs, best showcase who you are and what you do, and are attended by people who are in your target market.

As different opportunities arise, you need to ask yourself the following questions:

- How will this event help me advance my mission to reach my audience?
- Is my primary purpose at this specific venue to inform, teach, showcase knowledge, or entertain the audience?
- What kind of specific opportunities will I have to raise awareness about my products and services?
- Will the tone and the approach of the event align with who I am and what I do so the audience gets a chance to know me authentically?

Don't expect or demand a "Broadway debut." You may have oodles of natural talent and but there's a reason most actors start out in off-off-Broadway productions and that reason likely applies to you: a chance to tweak your content and develop your presentation techniques before you hit the majors. Your own off-off-Broadway appearances may include speaking at a Palmdale nonprofit, a Des Moines church group, a Memphis bookstore, or a Chicago café.

Plan to grow as you go. Seek out opportunities where you can successfully develop your repertoire and skills and celebrate each chance to become a seasoned speaker. Be sure to give every venue and every audience member the same effort you'd give to a Broadway production.

Remember less can be more. Who is there is more important than how many are there. Excellent promotional opportunities exist regardless of event size. A small group of passionate people can produce more results than an event comprised of hundreds of lukewarm folks.

How do you take it to the next level? To gain a competitive edge, you need to leverage any live event so that you also get media attention whenever you can. Remember, every live event placement you secure can be leveraged. Use each live event to gain bigger and better placements. When speaking out of town, secure invitations to be a guest on TV or radio by alerting local media of your availability. Enhance your image as a speaker by collecting event photographs, video clips, and press clippings to add to your inventory of promotional materials.

COACHING CLINIC #10

Live event opportunities exist at local, regional, and national levels. Your involvement can open all kinds of doors, including opportunities with print and broadcast venues. The important thing to know is that you can be strategic with your time and you can seek out what works best for you.

Consider:	Ask yourself these questions:
On any given day, you can find a Rotary meeting, a book club, a church group, a community center, a class, or a special interest organization that meets regularly. Any of these folks might enjoy your guest appearance if they simply understood the connection between you and their wants and needs. Live event opportunities exist at local, regional, and national levels.	What kind of live events interest you most?
You can utilize a local event to acquire print or broadcast media coverage. You can plan a live event to strategically enhance a particular window of opportunity for you.	What does the event coordinator need from you to help promote the event? Is the number of attendees, or the topic matter, or your participation newsworthy? Is the event appropriate for the calendar section of the local paper? Would the feature editor be interested in a broader topic with a local event tie-in?
Participating in live events can earn you the street credibility you need to impress your target audience.	How will you make sure your target market knows that you were chosen to be featured at this live event?

PR
PRESCRIPTION

CEO Myelita Melton is a trainer, speaker, voice coach for executives, and author of the SpeakEasy Spanish series (SpeakEasySpanish.com), the nation's leader in Spanish training. She offers the following advice to those wishing to speak to groups:

When it comes to speaking in front of a group, know your voice and its limitations:

- Record your material and listen critically to your voice. Are you monotonous? What words can you punch to add enthusiasm?
- Are you using pauses effectively?
- Do you vary the pace of your delivery and the pitch of your voice?
- Your voice should paint a picture of who you are. Vocal color is critical to good speaking.
- Before you begin your critical presentation, take a moment to be alone. Find a restroom stall. Focus and center your energy. Check your hair. Take three good, deep breaths. Then go hit a home run!

PHASE IV

Your PR Empowerment Tools

One of the most rewarding opportunities in my career came along a few years ago when I wanted to shift gears professionally, step back to write this book, and find a way to rediscover how my work could make a tangible difference at a deeper, more personal level.

But how was I to do this?

That's when I heard about a nonprofit in a suburb of Kansas City that needed some marketing expertise. From what I could find out, they were pretty gung ho about mental health. Yeah, mental health. I've always been fascinated by the mental health field and had some notable experience working on the West Coast with psychologists who were experts in depression, anger, grief, shyness, and more.

So, the opportunity to help this group caught my attention...in fact, it seemed like an answer to my prayers.

Based on the nonprofit's website, it looked to me to include a pretty solid, pretty compassionate bunch of folks who just needed some increased local awareness and an integrated marketing approach developed by someone who cared as much about marketing as they cared about wellness.

Turns out I was in for a few surprises.

First off, this little nonprofit was *not* little. In fact, it was five times bigger than I had perceived it to be. ReDiscover serves more than 500 people a day. This "little" nonprofit had quietly built some of the most unique and successful mental health and substance abuse programs in the state of Missouri. After a little nosing around, I met psychiatrists, psychologists, case managers, counselors and dozens of clients with incredible, heart-wrenching stories of suicide, depression, schizophrenia, bipolar disorder, drug addiction, and poverty. And, just when I thought I'd met them all, I found out that there were a whole bunch more still left to be met. Before long, I recognized that while ReDiscover was indeed doing exceptional work, its promotional tools were no longer doing it justice. In fact, its communication tools didn't begin to tell the real depth of its story, the real scope of its outreach. Suddenly, the marketing assignment I had initially hoped would be a one-year tour of duty turned into an indigenous Peace Corps-like personal mission.

One year turned in to two and then three, and that nonprofit became a charity of choice for me, professionally and personally, as I made friends with some of the most genuinely caring people I've ever met. From the president of the company to the receptionist at the front desk, the people who work at ReDiscover are tireless in their efforts to be a safety net for their clients and the community at large.

You don't have to be a nonprofit to take this bit of promotional insight away for yourself: When you love what you do and you're passionate about your work, a wonderful thing happens—you grow. The thing is, when you grow, you typically become so busy that you outgrow your communication tools—that is, one day the website, the images, and the written descriptions just don't fit who you are anymore. So, take a fresh new look in the mirror and make sure that you know who you really are now, and that what you do at the level where you are operating is represented accurately—not too modestly and not too over-the-top, just accurately, authentically, and like it really is. The right communication tools change everything.

SESSION ELEVEN
Scripting the Perfect Pitch

"How do I get an interview with a newspaper or magazine?"
"How do I get invited on a TV program or a radio show?"
"How do I get my foot in the door?"

Now that you've had a chance to really consider the scope of your opportunities, what's the best way to really get what you want? Believe it or not, the answer is simpler than you may imagine—ask for it.

Asking for what you want doesn't mean you must adopt the hard-sell tactics of a used car salesman or the thick-skinned persistence of a telemarketer. To get the attention of the media, adopting an unnatural style, a pushy demeanor, or some kind of phony approach will likely get you nowhere at all.

But, pitching a genuinely good idea to the right people is something else entirely. It's exciting and fun. So, mind your manners and follow the preferred protocol. Here are the five steps you need to understand the process of scripting and delivering the perfect pitch, whether you choose print, broadcast, or live venues as your target:

- Do your homework
- Focus on your pitch points
- Choose your approach
- Make contact
- Follow up.

Do your homework.
Your first order of business is to do the groundwork you need to do to set up effective meetings with decision makers who can make things happen. Start by identifying whom you really want to approach. Compile the list of appropriate newsroom staffers, beat reporters, producers, or live event coordinators.

Whether you have your eye on a print, broadcast, or live venue, know whom you want to talk to and why. Make notes on what you want, check your research, if necessary, about lead-time requirements, and know what you want to get out of every pitch.

Be clear about the specific goal for every person you plan to contact. Typically, your initial goal is to generate enough interest in your idea so your contact will agree to engage in discussing the idea in greater detail.

Focus on your pitch points

Make your message fitting and clear. Scripting the pitch is as easy as simply telling the truth with excitement. Nothing more, nothing less. Write out your idea as a quick script. You want a very brief summary that is clear, compelling, and intriguing:

- This is who I am.
- This is what I'm doing that will interest you.
- This is why I think you ought to know right now.

If you are calling, edit the initial "Hello" pitch down to no more than three sentences and have bulleted points for your beyond-hello details. If you are e-mailing, edit the pitch so that it's no longer than the length of the screen, presented in a reasonably sized font—no scrolling required. If you are writing a letter for regular mail, keep the proposal to one page.

Choose your approach

If the idea of picking up the phone to pitch yourself causes a panic attack, don't use the phone—try an e-mail instead; it's typically preferred. Take note: Many people access their e-mail on their phones and many phones have huge limitations when it comes to what info the person can see—keeping messages short is critical. If the thought of e-mailing feels awkward to you, write a letter. The conventional letter has become a stand-out-from-the-crowd novelty that garners more attention now than ever before—as long as the letter is received in time to make it feel relevant to the recipient.

A critical aspect to effective pitching is to develop a strong pitch strategy that balances your needs with your abilities. Striking a balance allows you to overcome the personal concerns, misconceptions, and private fears that are so often connected to promoting your work or yourself. Most important, understanding your needs and choosing a method that's personally comfortable allows you to focus more energy on developing your message to the highest level.

Make contact

You've done your homework. You've read the publication, watched the show, or you know something about the venue. You feel fairly confident about what would work and why your idea will resonate. Keep the pitch brief, so it will stand out. You're likely pitching to someone who gets dozens to hundreds to thousands of pitches each week by phone, by mail, by fax, and by e-mail. The last thing anyone needs is a rambling voice mail or multi-page pitch letter. Don't try to communicate everything there is to know, just enough substance to raise interest. It's only human to pick the items that seem both interesting and easy to understand. So, keep it focused—whether it's e-mail, telephone, or snail mail—on the following:

- Identify yourself.
- Explain why you're making contact.
- Provide the relevant who, what, where, when, and why.
- Ask for what you want.

Make it timely. News must be timely in order to be news. Reporters are always looking for a timely news angle, tied perhaps to some event, date, or anniversary. And think visuals. Nothing tells a story better than a terrific photo.

Consider the audience. Ask yourself, "What's the value to their audience?"

- Do assume your pitch is worth a reporter covering.
- Do be enthusiastic.
- Do be persistent and call back if you do not get in touch with the reporter right away.
- Don't pitch two reporters at the same news outlet at the same time.
- Don't argue with a reporter.
- Don't read a script.
- Don't call during the presentation of a big news story or at deadline time.
- Describe what access you can offer to people who are involved in the story.

Follow-up

Be prepared to respond to any request for more information, access to an authority for an interview, and whatever is needed to achieve the goal:

- The key is relevance and clarity.
- What is the *new* news?
- What are you providing to help reporters tell your story?
- Will there be fact sheets or interviews?
- What visuals will you use at your event?

COACHING CLINIC #11

Different people have different reasons for appreciating who you are and what you do. When you pitch an idea, it helps to stay focused and only share the most relevant facts and details to support your idea. When your goal is to deliver a strong pitch, you have to keep the chosen concept simple, clean, and clearly uncluttered. Create a core set of personal cue cards to make your most important messages simple and meaningful.

Fill in the following blanks to create your own 30-second pitch scripts:

Focused One-Sheet
Who is the target for this pitch?
Focus of pitch:
What is the main message?
What specific points would your contact like to learn about?
1.
2.
3.
How does my service, product, or book connect to this audience?
What info about me will resonate with them the most?
Add specific background info that applies.

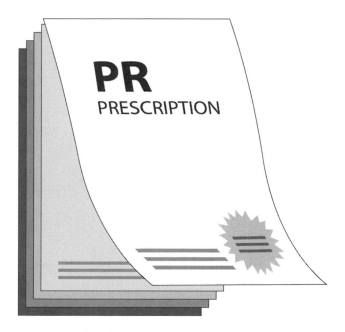

Beth Welsh, who is the community faces coordinator for the *Kansas City Star* **(CommunityFaces.kcstar.com), suggests you get the picture:**

Everybody wants to see what's going on, so don't forget the pictures:

- Shoot candid (unposed) photos, in addition to posed shots. Some people tense up when they know a camera is pointed their way, and they will look more relaxed and natural when photographed candidly.
- Fill the frame. Zoom in or get closer to your subject. Try to avoid including large areas of blank wall, grass, water, or other non-meaningful background.
- Use your flash outdoors as well as indoors. Fill flash, used outdoors, helps smooth out dark shadows on sunny days and adds sparkle on cloudy days.
- Take more than one shot of your person, group, or scene. It's insurance against closed eyes, no flash, or out-of-focus first shots.

SESSION TWELVE
Pumping Up Your Press Materials

"How do I make the right impression?"
"How do I wow the media without making anything up?"

Who are you? What do you do?
    You only have one chance to make a great first impression. So make the most of it. Tell your story. Answer those basic who-what-why questions cleanly and clearly. And, tell personal tale in a voice that is distinctly your own—in the best way the media can hear you: in writing.

Your press materials need to do the job they're supposed to do. What's their job? To make the media stop…look…and ask for more. The right communication tools can capture hearts, ignite imaginations, and mobilize people to help you spread the news about you and your products or services to *more* people who need to know.

So, do exactly what it takes to get things rolling.

Provide bite-size pieces of extraordinary detail. Vividly illustrate how and why you are relevant. And, don't you dare bury your info under clutter or mediocre messages. The goal here is to showcase the most interesting and relevant information in the least amount of words—and to do so with style.

You need to answer the following questions:

- Who are you?
- What do you do?
- What are the specifics of what you do?
- Do you have ready-to-serve information that is immediately usable by the audience?

Who Are You?

Start with the "Who are you?" part. Two of the most important communication tools you'll ever use are your bio/profile and your publicity photo.

The bio/profile is a brief, one- to two-page chronicle of the accomplishments relevant to your career. A *good* bio will tell who you are and what you've done. A *great* bio will reflect who you are and what you've done, *plus* generate the feeling that you're full of potential, already in perpetual motion, and on your way to the top or maintaining your spot there.

To start, you must recognize and believe that you are someone special. The truth is, you are special. You are special because you have a different background, a different perspective, and different goals than anyone else. The combination of who you are, what you've done, and where you're going makes you distinctly different. Different is important. Being different means you can bring something different to the table. Your bio needs to make it easy for people to see what that difference is and why that difference is so important. Your bio should reveal this in a matter-of-fact, clear, and concise way; avoid a tone of self-aggrandizement.

Acknowledge your accomplishments. Most people want to see if you have a track record. If you do not have any experience in your chosen field, get some. If you have to give your time away for a short period to acquire your credentials, consider it an investment in your career. If you have a zillion achievements, showcase them like the cluster of diamonds that they are.

Be honest. Banner-waving is fine; just make sure the information is accurate. Think of everything you have done that is related to your career. Everything. The hodgepodge of info can be tied together in a relevant way to show you're uniquely qualified for what you do. Think about hobbies, relevant degrees, unusual experiences, awards and recognitions, and, of course, your employment history.

Consider all your assets. Characterize your accomplishments in the best light possible, but always be prepared to stand behind everything you say. Characterize your achievements with hard facts. Think about stating facts that mention circulation, geographic location, population, ties to recognizable names, high-status elements, dollar figures, and any other applicable numbers. For example, "I work for a nonprofit" is not as strong as, "I work for a nonprofit that serves 500 people daily." Or, "I produced a radio show" is not as strong as, "I produced a radio show in Los Angeles County that had political guests who included the vice president of the United States."

Give people enough information to understand you. Make people want to know you and they will want to buy your products and services or refer others to you who will.

The publicity photo

Your official publicity photo is an important basic item. Up front, you need to take as much care in selecting the professional photographer as you later take selecting the right photo from the shoot. Choose a photo that will look good even when reduced down to the size of a postage stamp.

You are often judged by your photo, so you need to consider the tone you want to convey. Business-like? Casual? Zany? The photo needs to make an appropriate statement if or when it is used in the following:

- Your website
- Promotional brochures
- Packaging for products that could include books, CDs, or manufactured items
- Fliers advertising live-event appearances
- Press releases.

But a picture of you isn't the only publicity photo you may need with your press material. If you have a product, you also need a professional quality image of your product, so people can see exactly what you are talking about. You want a sharp, flattering photographic image that is not compromised by poor lighting, flash glares, or distracting backgrounds.

Remember, 72 dpi images are fine for use on the Web, but for print media they need to be 300 dpi.

What Do You Do?

Next, focus on the "What do you do?" part of the press materials. Two communication tools that will serve your basic needs are a Detailed Product/Service Overview and a General Interest Flyer.

- **The Detailed Product (or Service) Overview.** This is a brief description of your product or service that provides the pertinent information that customers need so they can buy your product or request a proposal for your service.
- **The General Interest Flyer.** This one-page description of your product or service is big on image and small on word count. This flyer serves as a teaser to ignite enough interest to get people to visit a website or ask for more information.

Each item of your promotional material needs to bear your contact information since they may become separated from each other.

What Are the Specifics?

Next, go for the "What are the specifics of what you do?" material. Two communication tools that will serve your basic needs are the Sample Interview Questions and the Talk Topic One-Sheet.

Sample Interview Questions. This is a short list of questions to help an interviewer who often will not have had the time to develop his own questions. This list can work to jump-start the conversation. Set the parameters around your comfort zone. The list can be as short as ten questions, or it could offer specific topic details with relevant questions for each area.

Talk Topic One-Sheet. This is a college-catalog-style listing that describes your potential at live events as a guest speaker, keynote speaker, seminar leader, panelist, or moderator, as well as setting the stage for media interviews. This also defines what listeners will learn when you speak on a topic.

Ready-to-Serve Information

Finally, direct your attention to the "Do you have ready-to-serve information that is immediately usable by the audience?" piece. Three communication tools that will serve your basic needs are the Q & A Article, the Tip Sheet, and the Live Event Handout:

- **The Q & A Article:** This is a list of intriguing questions and your quotable, succinct answers to them. It could be used as a stand-alone article or it could be cut up and used in a feature story that someone else writes. It offers quotable comments on topics that you commonly discuss. Your Q & A article also offers excellent material that can be offered to other bloggers if you decide to conduct a Blog Tour. The publishing industry has perfected the use of Blog Tours for authors with new books, but the cross-promoting premise is useful for anyone with important information to share. A Blog Tour encompasses connecting with bloggers you like and making plans to virtually tour specific blogs on specific days with your news, exchanging links between your site and each Tour Stop, being on hand to respond to comments from each audience during a particular time period, and perhaps offering a giveaway for each blogger's community to help raise excitement with blog audiences. A fast way to get things rolling is to share your Q & A article with the blog host when arrangements for the Blog Tour are hammered out.
- **The Tip Sheet.** This is a simple list that includes up-to-a-dozen useful tips. This is often a device to get thousands of dollars in free publicity. Here's an example:

PRTherapy.com's Five Tips to Create Your Own Tip Sheet

1. Use numbers in your headline. Numbers are interesting and tangible. "Five Steps," "Seven Ways," or "Ten Ideas" are all good.
2. Just tell your audience exactly what to do. Make it easy for them.
3. Be brief and straight-to-the-point. Limit the tips to no more than one page. Better yet, make the tips fit on a bookmark or on the back of your business card.

4. Design the tip sheet to be perfect for a sidebar or companion piece to a topic you talk about.

5. Don't worry about selling yourself in your tips. Let the title, the byline, or the bio credit handle the recognition. Just be sure that the credit mentions your website, so people can find you.

- The **Live-Event Handout.** This term refers to any material to be handed out to the audience at a live event. Handouts are often in flyer form. To save time, you may want to produce a standard handout to use at multiple events. Always include your website address, including a sentence that promises more information or other benefits that will be available to those who go to the site.

Press Material Boilerplate

Once you've developed your core communication tools, it's time to pick up the pace. The art of building your brand and your reputation requires a certain ability to move quickly. You have to be able to produce tailor-made press releases and pitch letters without starting from ground zero every single time you need to get out of the gate. Having press material boilerplate will expedite the process and reduce the possibility of conflicting details. The boilerplate copy will include a standard statement about you, your company, group, or program. The purpose is to quickly boil the information down to a few clear statements that need to be included in every outreach effort.

This boilerplate keeps the heart of your most important messages consistent and cohesive and yet allows you to create or update a new piece quickly with fresh lead-in paragraphs and unique details relevant to the situation at hand.

COACHING CLINIC #12

Tool Time! Using this easy-to-follow checklist, you will assess your own needs and make plans to create or overhaul the press materials you need most to put the *motion* into your pro*motion*al plans. Examples of the four most important tools are presented later in this chapter. To see samples of all these materials, visit PRTherapy.com.

Status			Item	Next Step	Deadline
Have	Need to Create	Need to Update			
			Bio/Profile		
			Personal Publicity Photo		
			Product Publicity Photo		
			The Detailed Product (or Service) Overview		
			The General Interest Flyer		
			The Sample Interview Questions		
			The Talk Topic One-Sheet		
			The Q & A Article		
			The Tip Sheet		
			The Live-Event Handout		
			Press Material Boilerplate		

Example of Bio/Profile

BIO / PROFILE

Robin@PRTherapy.com

ROBIN
BLAKELY

For more than a decade, Robin Blakely has provided PR therapy for people promoting products and services that include books, audio tapes, DVDs, computer software, nonprofit services, seminars, classes, and one-on-one consulting.

Author of PR THERAPY (Quill Driver Books / 2009), Robin has secured and managed promotional placements for clients at print, broadcast, and live venues that have included HGTV, Book TV, The *Los Angeles Times* Festival of Books, Printer's Row, The National Baseball Hall of Fame, *The Hollywood Reporter*, ABC World News, *Vanity Fair*, CBS The Early Show, Harvard's Kids Risk Symposium, NPR's *On Point*, and more. Robin has provided media coaching and executive coaching to clients participating in satellite media tours for Crest, Listerine, Similac, Huggies, QVC, and more. She has shepherded more than 100 fiction and nonfiction books into the marketplace, working through all phases of book development, sales, product launch, and author/book promotions in genres that include business, psychology, mystery, romance, science fiction, handcrafts, children's, how-to, parenting, humor, and more.

An advocate for nonprofit causes, Robin has launched and directed workshops, special events, volunteer programs, and promotional campaigns for causes that empower adults with developmental disabilities; the elderly; at-risk children, people with asthma, cancer, or mental illness; women and vocational rehabilitation; and overcoming stigmas of poverty. She writes a weekly newspaper column that focuses on mental health.

Earlier in her career, Robin was a news writer who became the producer of a live radio talk show that featured guests who included the vice president of the United States, best-selling authors including NY Times bestseller Harvey MacKay, comedians such as Bob Hope, Jeff Foxworthy, and Steve Allen, television personalities such as Mike Wallace, and award-winning authors, including such luminaries as Madeleine L'Engle, Jon Scieszka, Barbara Park, Patricia Polacco, and more. For seven years, Robin taught and coordinated the Professional Writers Certificate Program at California University Extension Services at California State University, Long Beach.

Robin now lives in the suburbs of Kansas City, MO with her handsome husband who cooks, three talented kids who love commercials, and the family's neurotic poodle who never sleeps at night. She is a partner at Get There Media, Inc, based in New York City, the founder of Livingston Communications, Inc., and the editor of www.PRTHERAPY.com.

Callout annotations:

Give the page a title so readers know what they are looking at when they receive it.

Make sure you include your contact info.

Give real samples—name and numbers—so it's very clear the level at which you're actually operating.

Showcase your real interests.

Don't forget the human touch. You have a real life!

One page is enough—even if Captain Kangaroo should have made the cut!

Example of a Detailed Product Overview

About the Books
Polly Pepper Mysteries by R.T. Jordan

The Polly Pepper Mystery series

www.PollyPepperMysteries.com

PW raves:
"...What if Carol Burnett had starred in Murder She Wrote?...the start of a promising series..."

Library Journal praises:
"...Full of Hollywood types bent on success and willing to do anything to get it, Jordan's zany, name-dropping tale is full of snide comments and vicious sniping at what has become the norm in the movie capital of the world. This is laugh-out-loud funny..."

PW raves again:
"...Jordan's second Polly Pepper mystery delivers a fun romp through the underworld of regional theater...Even among a cast of such well-developed, eccentric characters, Polly steals the show, drinking champagne constantly and even naming her mansion's staircase the Scarlett O'Hara Memorial Staircase. Jordan's entertaining plot moves briskly and its plucky heroine is sure to charm old fans and win new ones..."

Final Curtain
Second Book in the Series.
Polly Pepper, the legendary superstar of television's golden age, is finally back in the entertainment headlines. She's landed the title role in a new production of the musical Mame, and though it's off-off-off Broadway (Glendale, California, actually), Polly's bank account - and her ego - need the job. And if all goes well, the show just might go to New York! There's one minor detour though: on the second day of rehearsals, wunderkind director Karen Richards turns up dead. It'll take all of Polly's wits - and some help back at Pepper Plantation from her ever-dependable son Tim, and their perpetually wisecracking maid Placenta - to save the jailed soap star from a murder rap. Polly's adventure is filled with Tinseltown gossip, canoodling with suspects, champagne drinking, and hilarious mayhem. Kensington (2008) **ISBN-10:** 0758212828 **ISBN-13:** 978-0758212825

Remains to be Scene
First Book that Launched the Series. **Now available in Paperback!**
Living legend Polly Pepper is an icon from the Golden Days of television when she and other comedy stars like Lucille Ball and Carol Burnett ruled that corner of the entertainment world. Always wanting to get back into the limelight, even in a small part, Polly has a chance for a comeback when character actress Trixie Wilder dies in an unlikely accident on a movie set.
But, Polly's golden opportunity is snatched away by her worst nightmare, Sedra Stone, who not only steals this role, but has stolen two of Polly's husbands. When Sedra is murdered on the set, Polly gets two roles—one on-screen, and the other as an amateur detective leading an unofficial investigation with the help of her suave son Tim and her faithful wisecracking maid Placenta. This farce on the lifestyles of the rich and famous is filled with Hollywood egos and laced with pop culture references. Kensington; Reprint edition (2008) **ISBN-10:** 075621281X **ISBN-13:** 978-0758212818

Visit www.PollyPepperMysteries.com / www.RTJordan.com
For Author Interviews: contact Robin Blakely / Livingston Communications at 660-918-2723

Give each page a clear description so readers know what it's about.

Don't forget to highlight the praise your product has received. If you don't have rave reviews, ask for some from happy customers.

Be sure to visually profile the product so customers can recognize it when they see it.

Insert identifying info to help people order the product: an ISBN for a book or the model number for other products.

Make sure your contact info is in an easy-to-read place.

Example of a Sample Interview Questions Sheet/Short Version

SAMPLE INTERVIEW QUESTIONS

Label the page so everyone knows exactly what they are looking at.

ReDiscover
Help.....Hope.....Healing

ReDiscover is a nonprofit community mental health agency that offers a full spectrum of programs and services for people whose lives have been affected by mental illness and/or substance abuse.

Focus on topics that are especially relevant to you.

1. How Many People Did ReDiscover Serve Last Year?

2. What is ReDiscover's Service Area?

3. What's The Connection Between Mental Health Agencies, Hospitals, And Jails?

4. Do People With Mental Illness Get The Help They Need In Hospitals And Jails?

5. How Are School Children Affected By Mental Illness?

6. What Kinds Of Stereotypes Impact Children With Mental Illness?

7. How Can People Help Fight The Stigma Of Mental Illness?

8. How Can People Help ReDiscover Help The Community?

9. If ReDiscover Had An Extra $100,000, What Projects Would The Agency Start Or Expand?

10. What Should You Do If You Know Someone Who Is In Crisis or Needs Help Managing a Mental Illness?

www.rediscovermh.org

Find ways to offer tips or steps to help with problems that your audience may have.

Add your website whenever you can, in case one page gets lost from the rest of the press material. Provide descriptors. On a cluttered desk, scattered press papers may be difficult to identify.

Example of the Sample Interview Questions Sheet/Longer Version

SAMPLE INTERVIEW QUESTIONS

ReDiscover
Help.....Hope.....Healing

Alan Flory, President / CEO of ReDiscover

ReDiscover's mission: *"To deliver mental health and substance abuse services to help individuals and families achieve healthier and more productive lives."*
ReDiscover is a nonprofit community mental health agency that offers a full spectrum of programs and services for people whose lives have been affected by mental illness and/or substance abuse. ReDiscover helps men, women, and children, including those who have limited income, no insurance, or who are under-insured.

SAMPLE INTERVIEW TOPICS& QUESTIONS

1. What are the Urgent Funding Needs for Community Mental Health?
Alan can discuss why Community Mental Health facilities across the Kansas City metro and throughout the state need *more* funding, *not* funding cuts. When our government officials neglect and ignore community mental health needs, Emergency rooms and jails are being placed at-risk.
- *What's The Connection Between Mental Health Agencies, Hospitals And Jails?*
- *Will The Mentally Ill Get The Help They Need In Hospitals And Jails?*
- *What Do You Think Is Really At Stake Here?*

2. How are School Children affected by Mental Illness?
Alan can discuss common questions parents have about children and mental illness. ReDiscover offers services for all ages, including families and children. We serve children in our office buildings as well as on many local school campuses, and even through in-home visits to the child's house. ReDiscover also operates one of the only transitional living programs in the state specializing in youth with mental illness.
- *How Common Are Mental Health Disorders In Young People?*
- *Can Mental Illness In Children Be Prevented?*
- *What Are Common Treatment Options For School Children?*
- *What Kinds Of Stereotypes Impact Children With Mental Illness?*

3. Are There Ways to Help Friends, Family, and the Community?
Alan can discuss what people can do to help their friends and family members who are living with mental illnesses...and he can share ways to help make a difference in the community for those who would like to get involved. ReDiscover relies on volunteers to help stretch our scarce resources. Over 300 volunteers donate 6,000 hours annually to ReDiscover. Charitable gifts help us guide families toward recovery. Private financial assistance allows us to offer more services like rapid response to hospitals, domestic violence shelters, and the local police.
- *What If People Know Someone Who Needs Help?*
- *How Can People Fight The Stigma Of Mental Illness?*
- *What About People Who Want To Help Rediscover Help The Community?*

Label the page so people know what they are looking at.

Provide just the basic info about who will be interviewed (more details are on the bio/profile). Offer some interesting and relevant facts.

Clarify the specific topics you could discuss and provide questions that can jumpstart the interview.

Make it easy for the person interviewing you to sound knowledgeable. Cluster key facts with a topic and its questions.

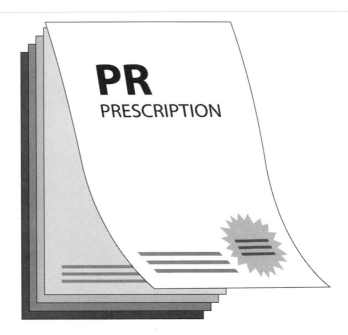

R.T. Jordan is a Disney Studios publicist, as well as a novelist and film and music producer. His list of suggestions below provides good advice to both pros and novices:

1. **Neatness counts.** If you want to be a professional, act like one. Your press kit, press releases, and cover letters are a reflection of who you are. Look sharp.
2. **Don't rely on spell check.** Your computer is not to blame for typos, you are. Always have another pair of eyes review your work.
3. **If you're going to lie, get your facts straight.** If you claim that you attended the Juilliard school, for heaven's sake, make sure you spell "Juilliard" correctly.
4. **Knock off the hyperbole.** When writing your bio, don't put yourself on a pedestal. Let others do that for you.
5. **Promises, promises.** If you can't be a man of your word, let your clients know as soon as possible.
6. **Never miss a deadline.** Unless you're dead.
7. **Keep your bio to one double-spaced page.** Save your likes and dislikes and your purple prose for your on-line dating/cheating profile.
8. **Spend the money on professional photos.** Lighting is everything.
9. **Attention deficit disorder, everybody has it.** So get straight to the point. And keep your sentences short.

SESSION THIRTEEN
Heating Up Your Database

"How do I get a good contact list?"
"How do I keep all my info organized so I can use it?"

W e've all heard the old maxim: "It's not what you know, it's who you know." In promotions, the greater truth is this: "It's not who you know, it's how you organize who you know."

Many PR seekers experience a flash of panic when they suddenly realize that a mailing list they purchased, combined with a hodge-podge of business cards collected over the years and a bunch of phone numbers and e-mail addresses scribbled on Post-It-Notes, is not exactly an easy system for keeping important contact information at their fingertips.

If you are one of these people, it will be a relief to discover that some simple organizational strategies can move you forward in a big way. It is possible to transform the wildest collection of names into a powerful communication tool that you can use to drive business your way. And, perhaps most importantly, you don't have to race out and buy the most sophisticated, complicated, and expensive piece of database software to start making real results happen.

If you're a one-man or one-woman show or if you're an under-budgeted nonprofit or a struggling small business, you already know you have to work smarter than everyone else to meet your commerce goals. You can't afford to waste time, energy, or money on tasks that don't connect to your bottom line.

So, let's look at that bottom line as it relates to promotional outreach.

When considering your next promotional message, you should be able to pinpoint a clear purpose for that message and an anticipated response from its recipients.

As you reach out to media and get drawn into the busy flurry of their landscape, it is easy to lose sight of the original need to approach them. Your media contacts may be the first recipients of your promotional message but they are not your most important recipients. Your promotional messages are supposed to ultimately reach your target market audience of Hardcores, Newbies, or Other Guys.

Knowing whom each message is meant to reach and deciding what action you want the members of each group to take when they receive your messages is extremely critical. You need to choose the end destination and the best method to get there before you even compose the message. Your database of contacts needs to readily serve as the railroad tracks for the delivery of your message.

With this in mind, a thoughtfully organized database of key contacts allows you to quickly reach out to the people you want, when you want, and how you want. You need to consider how you and your various contacts may prefer to communicate:

- Will you mail press releases and news alerts?
- Will you send e-mail blasts?
- Do your contacts prefer to be reached by phone and voice mail?
- By fax?
- By Skype?
- By Twitter?
- Through LinkedIn, MySpace, or Facebook?
- By e-newsletter?

As you consider the possibilities of how you will communicate, you have to also consider how to tailor your database infrastructure so that you can use it to meet your business needs and meet everyone's communication preferences. The way you manage your database of key contacts must match how you think, so you will intuitively know how to add new names and how to locate them again when you need them.

Selecting the Right System

The technology that you choose to keep your contacts organized needs to match your personal skill sets. You cannot be burdened by tools so sophisticated that you are unable to operate them. You cannot afford to become buried under tons of unmanaged information. You cannot allow good contacts to get lost in database chaos.

In this session, we're going to focus on making sure you are organizing your contacts in an intuitive way that will help you move forward, not just promotionally, but also in a way that helps achieve your marketing and sales goals. We'll look at the types of names you need, the details you need to collect, and the foundational understanding required to create and sustain your database of contacts.

We'll walk through the prep stages of organizing your contacts so you can find the appropriate technology to support your unique plans, big or small. So, unless you already have a terrific outreach system, your next step is to shift gears and tame the names of all your contacts. If you don't yet know the right folks or don't yet know as many people as you need to know, this is your chance to assess your needs and to do what it takes to meet them.

First, we'll take a fresh look at your complete business communications structure. This encompasses taking a wider view than just looking at your need for media contacts. This is about reviewing all of your contacts and lining up three specific groups. You may find that you have names that just don't fit into the three categories; if so, set those contacts aside and keep your focus on building the three core groups that need to be operational in order for your success to become mobilized.

Here's a snapshot of the three groups of people who you need to organize and manage:

1. Customers: Hardcores, Newbies, and Other Guys
2. People in the media: print, broadcast, and Internet
3. Marketing and sales prospects: leaders at key venues that offer sales transaction opportunities for your products or services.

Organizing customers

Let's start with customers, your target audience of Hardcores, Newbies and Other Guys. In the database of your dreams, you will have collected contact information for all of your customers. With encouragement and communication from you, many customers can become key influencers who will increase grassroots interest in who you are and what you're doing. They will tell the people they know about you because they like you and they want to help others who may need you.

A service like ConstantContact.com is an easy way to reach out to your customers by e-mail. The service is inexpensive and it does more than e-newsletter outreach. It also offers easy template formats that can be customized with your own logos and pictures and set up as sales announcements, coupons, invitations, and more. ConstantContact and other services that are similar will allow you to include hyperlinks back to your website or blog. And it's super easy to group your contacts for specific campaigns with messages designed to resonate with specific recipients. Best of all, you can monitor the success of your outreach by viewing reports that show who opened your e-mails and who didn't.

You must build relationships with your customers, know who they are, and be able to reach them. In many cases, these customers will reach out to you through your own blog, website, and personal e-mail. When they do, you need to be able to capture their contact information and add it to your customer list so that you can communicate with them whenever you have special news, such as the release of a new product or service or if you want to share some general information that would be helpful to them.

Organizing the media

Next, let's think about developing your list of people in the media. As you go along, you must cultivate ways to access new customers. Naturally, a great help with this is being featured in newspapers, on radio and TV shows, and on Internet sites that your customers enjoy.

As you build your database of key contacts, you must lay the railroad tracks to your audience by selecting media to communicate with carefully. You have to keep an eye to reaching the specific audiences you want to reach. Your publicity goals are to reach members of the media who have the power to reach your target market with news about you and your products and services. Media exposure will impact your bottom line by setting the stage for marketing and sales efforts.

Organizing prospects

Finally, let's explore your marketing and sales prospects. Many PR seekers discover that it pays to develop a database that focuses specifically on marketing and sales prospects. That is, to increase sales, you have to raise awareness about yourself to those who can directly impact your marketing and sales goals. If you aren't sure who your marketing and sales prospects are, follow the money trail.

For example, if you're a speaker who is popular with parents of school-age kids, your audience is parents. But, some of your key marketing and sales prospects are decision makers at the schools who can invite you to come and talk to those parents. Your marketing and sales prospects are also the retail store managers and event coordinators who host back-to-school-nights and will sell your products to parents. Your marketing and sales prospects are people who provide a venue where sales transactions of your products and services can occur.

Early on, you may lump your marketing and sales prospects in with your list of customers or your list of people in the media. As you grow, it tends to expedite the growth of business if you find ways to share timely information about your products or services with your marketing and sales prospects in advance to increase sales to your audience. If you neglect to communicate with this group, an important link in your development process will remain disconnected and in a dormant mode.

How to Use Your System

With a renewed sense of who you must ultimately reach communications-wise, your next step is to make everything work both strategically and technically. As you now fully realize, you must control your outreach efforts with precision and meaning. Your messages need to be as personally relevant to each group of recipients as you can possibly make them.

Start by sorting people into the three core groups discussed above. If you don't organize your contacts into relevant groups, you're wasting your time and theirs. Both you and everyone you contact deserve a return for the investment of time and attention. Set aside names that fit none of these three categories. Your goal is to build the three core areas of contacts so that you have a powerful communication tool that will operate smoothly when you need it.

Collecting additional details

Beyond names, what details should be collected to build a useful database? It's easy to become overwhelmed. You may feel compelled to collect too much information in case you need it, or you may end up shortchanging yourself by collecting too little. Some PR seekers know that they cannot afford to allocate funds for mailing printed material, so they opt out of collecting details like mailing addresses. Others will not use a fax, so they don't bother storing fax numbers. Some have intriguing visions that involve Skype, so asking for Skype information becomes a priority for them while it would never be for others.

Below are the basic details that you will need to collect for each contact in your database. As you brainstorm your own communication strategies, you should review the basic detail elements and tailor them to meet your specific communication needs before you begin building your contact lists:

- First Name
- Last Name
- Job Title
- Company
- Address
- City
- State
- Zip
- Website
- E-mail
- Phone
- Notes

How many contacts are enough?

The quantity of names in the different areas of your database is uniquely yours to determine. Depending on who you are and what you do, the nature of your customer base could be very big or very small, include only people you have had current contact with, or include those dating back a decade or more. In addition, your marketing and sales prospects are also unique to who you are. As you begin to organize your key contacts, you will find that they may be located in one geographic area or scattered across several states or countries.

As for your list of people in the media, there are some general rules of thumb to consider about how many and what kind of names to collect. You could shoot for a million names, but you don't need a million. A regional media list could easily have seventy-five names—eventually about a dozen will matter most to you. For national media, 350 names would not be too many. But, truth be known, eventually you will routinely encounter and hope to cultivate meaningful relationships with a much smaller group—perhaps forty-five people or so—whom you will closely watch, contact, and eventually get to know pretty well.

You need to develop your media database with the objective of creating a strong mix of media contacts. That means that you need to make sure you are getting to know a healthy balance of people from the following sorts of organizations:

- Newspapers
- Radio stations
- Television stations
- A-list bloggers and podcasters.

Where do you get names?
You build a custom database of media contacts by doing some legwork:

• **Think newspapers.** To get rolling, check out the website USNPL.com, where you can type in your state and find links to virtually every newspaper in the region. You want to get to know the local editors and reporters in the area where you live, the area you grew up in, and the areas where you plan to travel. But don't just think locally; collect contact names of national columnists and reporters who cover your subject.

• **Think magazines.** Check out WoodenHorsePub.com, where you can access key contacts for consumer and trade magazines for the price of a cup of coffee. You can choose who might appreciate your information. The research work has all been done for you and laid out in an easy-to-read format that is constantly updated. Check out MediaBistro.com, where a cheap subscription will allow you to review current magazine mastheads and read up on pitching preferences from people in-the-know.

• **Think radio.** Check out the website Radio-Locator.com to track down radio stations by format category. You want to hook up with stations that cater to listeners that are part of your demographic audience.

• **Think TV.** Check out the website Newslink.org to consider geographic locations for TV stations in the areas where you live or will be traveling.

• **Think Internet.** Google has a blog search feature (BlogSearch.Google.com) that will direct you to blogs that recently discussed your topic. Another blog search resource is Technorati.com. Use the RSS feature available with most blogs to help you easily follow the discussion. For information on RSS and how to make the most of it, visit WhatIsRSS.com.

Of course, the local library is a worthwhile resource for research. It helps to review firsthand the newspapers and journals which are read by your target audience.

A reference book that is widely used throughout the public relations industry is the *News Media Yellow Book*. This directory is excellent—and expensive. You may find one at your local library or a university's library. The purchase price is worth the investment, but it may be more machine than you need at this stage of the game. The best way to know is to hold one in your hands and imagine the possibilities. Figure out how to use it before you buy it.

Meanwhile, tune in to what's going on. It's high time for you to follow the media coverage of your issues in the news. Chances are you need to know the people who are writing and producing pieces that show up in the news and chances are you probably should know the people who are featured in the pieces.

Google Alerts (Google.com/Alerts) can help you discover new contacts by tracking what's being reported and who is doing the reporting. (Don't forget to put your own name into a Google Alert to keep track of your own press hits.)

With so much information accessible to you from the comfort of your computer chair, don't forget the most important way to cultivate contacts for your database: Get personal—go out and shake some hands. It's important to make personal contacts as often as possible. It may seem too obvious to consider, but don't forget to carry your business card with you and remember to ask for the business cards of people you meet.

Train yourself to write notes on the back of the business cards you collect so you can remember which John Somebody was the John Somebody you promised to send more information by e-mail.

Those phone numbers in your cell phone and addresses in your e-mail contacts comprise the group of people most commonly forgotten during outreach efforts. Ask the people you know who they know. Ask them specifically for names of people they know in the media.

When you tell them what you are doing and what you need, your friends and colleagues can be amazingly forthcoming. When you do contact someone who has been personally referred to you, you are likely to get more attention. Give people who believe in you a chance to help you by offering you referrals that will make you stand out.

Managing your contacts

Getting names is not enough. You must manage them.

You may have tons of information washing over you on a daily basis. Business cards that trickle in from random encounters and those that come in like flash floods when you attend a scheduled event are only one source of leads. You may have contact information arriving by snail mail, by fax, or by e-mail. Your own handwritten notes when you talk on the phone may be another source. You need to capture this information and transfer details to the appropriate area of your database.

Getting into a routine at this stage is critical because no matter how much you personally grow or how sophisticated your database management becomes, you will always have to deal with an influx of paper every time you go to an event or take down a phone number when talking on the telephone.

E-mails often contain contacts that should also be formal entries in your database. You may also have files full of information listing media contacts that you have researched online but haven't done anything about. And, you probably have a notepad that has names of people scribbled on it that you aren't even sure why you originally wrote down.

What kind of technical skills do you need for success? Appropriate technology can make or break you. Be careful to avoid technology overkill. Having software that can do tricks is pretty pointless if you're stopped dead in your tracks because you don't have enough time in your day to learn how to operate the software.

Appropriate technology means you need the right tools for the job...your job...for your needs...for your skill sets. Think of it like this: You don't need a riding lawn mower if your yard is only the width of a push lawn mower. Likewise, you don't need powerful software to manage a database with only a few dozen names. By the same token, if you have thousands of names, don't try to keep up with them on handwritten index cards. There's a better way.

Right now, you have some important decisions to make about database management. One of those decisions is about coming to terms with the learning curve of managing your own database. Many people are confronted with the reality that their database needs are really at a much higher level than their required skill sets. This is the place where many people mutter, "This database thing is becoming a full-time effort. I have to focus on what I do, not on becoming a computer tech."

Learning how to build and operate your database doesn't have to get in the way of doing what you do. In fact, you cannot afford for it to. At this stage, you can either learn how to perform or learn how to permanently delegate your database chores. Or, you can temporarily delegate the database duties until you have a chance to learn how to operate the process at your own pace.

There are a number of database software choices you can explore. You need to understand your own needs and recognize your own expectations as you explore your options. Some software is overly large, hard to use, and more expensive than you may want. If you only want to connect by e-mail, consider ConstantContact. com. They have sign-up banners and forms you can place on your website that help you grow your contact list.

Before you dive deep into exploring software options, you need to feel comfortable answering these questions:

- How many contact names do you have now?
- How big will your database become in the next three months? In the next year?
- What communication preferences do your contacts or contact groups have?
- How often will you communicate with your contacts?

When it's time to choose your method of organizing your details, ask yourself these questions:

- What kind of computer operating system do I use?
- Who will be extracting information from and adding information to the database?
- Who will be responsible for maintaining the data?
- How often will the data be modified?
- Who will make these modifications?
- How will material be updated each year?
- In what ways can the database be maximized for outreach efforts?

The reality is, keeping database information up-to-date will eat up good chunks of someone's time. It's essential that both the paper part and the software part are controlled. Don't allow yourself to be tripped up by tedious detail. When tailored to meet your unique needs and to match your particular skill level, your database will do more than pull its own weight as a key part of keeping you in business.

Being successful at a communications outreach strategy is about as miraculous, confusing, and completely possible as planning a train trip across the country. The efforts may seem daunting, but when the train tracks are in place, the journey can be made.

COACHING CLINIC #13:

For most people, the clerical chore of keeping a database is tedious. For many, the technical issues are confusing; for others, the daily paper trail is problematic. Take a close look at where you stand in the process and consider ways to make progress.

STAGE/ PHASE	DEVELOPING Handwritten Phase	OPERATIONAL Electronic Phase	ADVANCING Magic of Mail Merge Phase	EXCELLING Special High Tech Software Phase
DATA COLLECTION PROCESS	Contacts are randomly collected. These people usually stumble on to you or you stumble on to them. You're usually surprised and pleased to find each other.	Contacts are mostly randomly collected, but some are proactively acquired. An informal process is developing for identifying and collecting contacts but it is not necessarily based on big-picture goals and objectives.	Contacts are equally acquired through both proactive efforts and random opportunities. A formal process is coming together for the identification, selection, and collection of contacts based on your goals. This level of organization allows you to tap into new outreach efforts such as Mail Merge, a way to fully personalize mail and email messages and quickly deliver individualized messages to your contacts list.	Contacts are mostly proactively acquired. A formal ongoing process is based on set goals and includes ongoing evaluation and development of process.
NAME SEARCH TECHNIQUES	When you need to find a particular name, phone number, or email address, you literally have to hunt through pants pockets and piles of paper to find the info.	When you need to find someone, you do a search on your computer. You have found a routine way of tracking your contacts electronically. Some key information may still be missing, but chunks of it are there.	You have become more sophisticated and thorough at structuring your data. Most key information is available for every contact.	When you need to find someone, you can search for a name by name or other unique info as well as by date of original contact, or date of last contact, or a keyword or category.
GOAL TO REACH	Set up a standard place to dump all incoming scraps of info into one box to be organized later. One big messy pile is better than dozens of little messy piles. Think about going digital.	Simply corral the info digitally. Transfer business card details, handwritten notes, and research info you've collected into an electronic format, even if it's as basic as a grocery-list style Word document.	Organize your list into a format that makes the information more structured. Divide the details into basic fields that include Company, Contact Name, Address, Phone Number, E-mail, Notes.	Maximize the capabilities of high tech tools and toys. A business card scanner works wonders. Certain software can do reports that guide future promotional choices and strategies based on past histories.

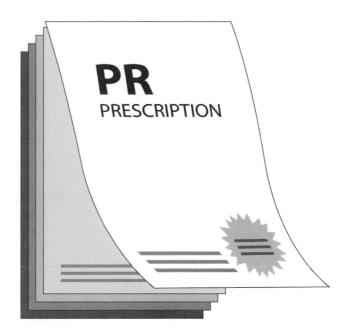

Mark Stroginis is the marketing director of Livingston Communications, a publicity company for new writers, artists, and creative talent. He has some creative advice for building your database:

How many times a day do you receive an e-mail, read a magazine article, look over a blog, or read a news report on CNN, MSN, or your favorite home page and see the name of the person who wrote it? If you think that person needs to know about your project, then contact them.

But how?

You already know the company name and their name, so the e-mail address is often easily located. Don't miss an important database-building opportunity. It's time to create a habit of copying and pasting the information right into your personal database.

I don't like to tear out articles or take the magazine from the doctor's waiting room. So, when I come across a contact in an article that I just have to have, I pull out my cell phone and leave myself a recorded memo. When I'm back at my computer, I just play the memo back and add the information to my database. If your phone isn't equipped with voice memo, send a text message to your e-mail address—it takes longer, but it's just as effective.

PHASE V

The Media and Doing What It Takes

Doing what it takes is never easy. All kinds of things can happen, and here are two that make me laugh now, although not so much at the time they happened.

We had an author with a humorous how-to book scheduled to do a presentation at a bookstore. Everything had come together as hoped. The store had actually kept its promise to feature her in its newsletter and to hand out promotional flyers to customers. She got a timely spot in the local newspaper, her event signage was showcased in the store's windows and its aisles, and, on event night, more than a dozen chairs were lined up in front of a linen-clothed table with a fresh flower and a mountain of her books.

Then, at the appointed hour, a mortifying thing happened—nobody came. Minutes ticked by and then the *next* mortifying thing happened—*one* person came. The client whispered to me, "What do I do now? And, oh geeze, what will I tell everyone later?"

The "now" part was easy, on with the show, but keep it short and make it personal. The "later" part, as it turned out, was covered too. We took a close look at the lone guy surrounded by empty chairs. As fate would have it, her one-man audience was a well-known stand-up comedian. Thereafter, when anyone asked how it went, we could truthfully declare: "Well, we were stunned by the turnout—we couldn't believe this, but *Sinbad* was there!"

Another client of mine had his heart set on the grand marshal role for an upcoming parade. The big problem was, we kept getting trumped by a popular rival. No matter what situation presented itself, this rival seemed to be four steps ahead of us, consistently snagging top billing and stealing every opportunity that came our way.

Looking back on it now, it's easy to understand that my client was a lone man up against the grinding Hollywood machine.

At the time, *Turner and Hooch* movie posters were everywhere—you know the one with a young Tom Hanks, in the same era as *Splash,* paired with a large slobbery French mastiff instead of a mermaid. Today you can see this poster in chain restaurants like Red Robin or Applebee's. My client would point at one of the *Turner and Hooch* posters and say, "How can I compete with that?"

The funny thing is, it wasn't Tom Hanks that was giving my client grief. In this case it was Hanks' sidekick Hooch, the big red mastiff, who was stealing my client's career opportunities.

The key for both of these clients was that they stayed in the fray and did whatever it took to succeed. One went on to have a best-selling book and the other went on to be grand marshal at many a parade. Doing what it takes can mean surviving a painful and humbling experience, like playing to an audience of one or learning to overcome professional jealousy or career envy with someone as unlikely as a canine celebrity. It's not always easy, but you can find your way. Keep moving forward. One step at a time.

Print Interviews

*"I just got an e-mail from an editor wanting an interview...
how do I prepare fast?"*

Whenever you are contacted for an interview, you must respond quickly or you may lose the opportunity.

This means at least the same day or, hopefully, the same half-hour. Reporters are almost always working with a tight deadline. One brief minute to you is an excruciating dog year to them. They want to talk to you *immediately*.

Don't forget, you aren't the only person they can interview. If you aren't available for an interview, well, someone else will be and they don't have time to lose waiting to see what will happen with you. They have to get their story turned in on time.

If you want to be quoted, you need to be available to give a quote.

This doesn't mean that you always have to speak off-the-cuff. Nor does it mean that you always have to be available to be interviewed at the drop of a dime or when you're really not prepared to focus on the interview.

Working with Reporters

So how do you do what they want *and* get what you need? First, respond to the reporter immediately. When speaking to him, take notes about what he needs so you have something to refer back to in case, when you get off the phone, fear sets in and your mind snaps off like a malfunctioning computer monitor.

Quickly find out some general information, including the interviewer's deadline, when and where the interview needs to be conducted, and what kind of information the reporter hopes you will provide. The key here is *quickly*. The reporter is likely in time-crunch mode.

Here are some questions you could ask:

- **What kind of deadline are you under?** Not every reporter will need to talk to you the same day or even the next day, but most will. Their turnaround time may be very short. The longer they have to wait to talk to you, the less time they have to work on writing the piece. It is okay to buy yourself some time to clear your schedule or calm your nerves, but don't make them wait too long. Don't get miffed if their tone is terse, curt, or sounds like their pants are on fire. Their pants *may be* on fire.
- **Do you want to interview me in person or handle it on the phone?** If geography allows, some reporters prefer to interview you face-to-face. They may take notes on a notepad. They may use a microphone and record your conversation. Others will want to talk on the phone. If you have a choice—and you may—choose what is most comfortable for you. As awkward or time-consuming as it may seem, you will make a bigger impact if you meet the reporter face-to-face. People are more likely to remember you for the next article if they've established personal contact with you. In the PR world, it helps for people to remember you.
- **What is the scope of the story?** If you know where the piece is headed, it is easier for you to provide relevant details. And, from the personal side, if you know going in that you can meet their expectations, you'll feel more comfortable and you'll have more fun.
- On the flipside, if you absolutely can't comply with a request or know you aren't a good fit for the proposed content, say so immediately, and the reporter will admire your honesty and professional demeanor. It's cool when you do what's right, what's best for the project, instead of taking a me-me-me attitude.
- **What kind of information do you hope I will provide?** Don't belabor this. But, it's okay to ask. You're just troubleshooting. What you really want to listen for is if they want information that needs to be compiled or collected. Don't offer to provide this stuff unless you have the information at your fingertips or are willing to research it. If you have the data—and it's okay to provide it for public consumption—offer it up like candy.
- **When can we arrange to do the interview?** Be straight up. Say something like, "Here's what I can do; what will work for you?" This kind of approach is appropriate. Be accommodating. Be as flexible as you can be. For the most part, no one is asking you to turn your life upside down in order to do the interview. Still, you win points if you're accommodating and likable.
- **How much time do you need for me to set aside for the interview?** If you know how much time the reporter wants to spend with you, it will help you pace yourself. Plan to be available five to ten minutes early and to stay fifteen to thirty minutes late. Most reporters are timely, but life can get in the way on a hectic news day. Wiggle room is usually much appreciated.

Be Prepared

Before the interview, prepare a list of main points to try to share. Of course, you must share the basic details:

- your name and title
- your website address and phone number
- ways the public can find out more about your service, product, and/or your company.

What should your other points be? Your points will largely depend on the audience and the reporter. Who you are and what you do somehow connect to the article the reporter is planning to write. The reporter has a vision for that article and knows how you will fit into the telling of the tale. You want to make sure the audience finds out who you are and what you do, but the reporter's agenda is never to sell more products and services for you. The reporter's agenda is to inform the audience of a story in which you are a legitimate part. Do what you can to connect the dots between yourself and the article's topic for the reporter and for the reporter's readers.

Cover the basics with flair. Have sharp, ready answers for these questions:

- **What do you do?** Make sure you frame your answer to connect with your audience's needs. They don't just want to know what you do. They really want to know how and why what you do matters to them. Tell them. Frame your answer so that the information you share illuminates the connection between what you do and why they need what you do. Try forming an answer that starts with "I help people by…."
- **Why do people need that?** Don't let the confrontational quality of this question throw you for a loop. Welcome the chance to get to the point. Try coming up with a response that starts with, "People come to me when they have problems with…" or "The people who are interested in what I am doing want me to…."
- **What makes you different?** Use this type of question as an opportunity to leverage the power of the marketplace and set your status. If you can drop names accurately and relevantly, include them by sharing what they have told you that will help answer the question. Consider framing your answer with: "The three things that I hear most often from my clients about what makes me so different are…" or "When I worked with Mr. Big Name, I was told that what made me so different is the way I…."
- **How did you get started in that?** Don't let your answer to this question become a story that rambles in a long-winded and pointless way. Don't waste time on story parts that are distracting or unimpressive. "I've been dreaming of writing plays since second grade…" or "My seventh grade English teacher

told me I'd be a writer." Try to fast-forward past the long, boring stuff. Pause only on the relevant bits by saying stuff like: "The moment I knew I'd do what I'm doing now happened like this…" or "Things really got rolling for me when this happened…."

During the interview, listen. Don't rush. Keep your answers simple. Don't say "No comment." Don't speak "off the record." And don't ever lie, even if it seems like bending the truth wouldn't matter. It does matter. Anything you say that is not technically true will bit you in the butt when you least expect it. You can prevent that by never lying.

What if you sense that you are really screwing up? If you become concerned about the way you're answering a question, remember you have the option to simply stop. Take a deep breath and put on the brakes. Gather your thoughts. You want to get it right. But do be aware that the reporter will notice your discomfort, is likely to be intrigued by it, and will possibly choose your original phrasing over a processed, less colorful second-attempt response.

The reporter's job is to give an accurate account of the story at hand. If you said it, it's ethically fair game to repeat your remarks. Being accurate is the reporter's creed. A way to regain some modicum of potential control over this sort of situation is to say, "Let's stop. I need to be more accurate. A more accurate response to your question is this…." The word *accurate* is a meaningful word to most reporters and will at least make them consciously consider choosing one set of remarks over another. Every reporter wishes to be accurate, but, like most things in life, accuracy can be a matter of opinion.

What if the reporter requests a response by e-mail? Sometimes a reporter will send a couple of questions to you and ask for a reply by e-mail. If you subscribe to a paid service like ProfNet or a free service like Peter Shankman's HelpAReporter.com, you may have the opportunity to respond to many different requests for articles that journalists across the country are writing. Respond to e-mail opportunities with quick, pithy replies. Be fast, be brief, and be quotable. Clearly connect your responses to the reporter's needs.

When responding by e-mail, follow this five-point format:

1. **You asked about this:** Bring them up to speed. Remind them what they wanted so that all the details are together and they don't have to try to remember what they asked about. Their days are often long and intense and they may be juggling a variety of cryptic e-mail strings. When they are pelted by a storm of a hundred e-mails a day, they appreciate the ease of looking at yours and being able to jump right in where they left off without trying to remember or figure out what the two of you were talking about or why they ever wanted what you seem to be sending. (One way to do this is to include the person's original e-mail in your response and type your direct

replies right below each question. Be sure to use a different font color so your remarks stand out. Clarity is king here, but if you choose to do this, watch your tone. In an attempt to be clear, your responses can sound so clipped, curt, or unintentionally rushed that you come off seeming arrogant and annoyed. Keep things warm and always make sure your greeting is friendly and that it explains that the responses exist within the original e-mail.)

2. **Here's my quote:** Give them a remark immediately usable for their piece. Your quote should be simple, direct, and memorable. Put it in quotation marks. Most should be only a few lines long. And, make sure the quote is completely on-topic. It should be directly tied to what you were asked about.

3. **About me:** Give them a phrase that identifies you that can be easily used in the piece. Give your full name and title as it should appear in the article. If you have several titles, make the titles short. Save this blurb for future use because you will need it again and again. It would be good to get a mention of your website in the article, so do it by saying something like "...author of XYZ book and creator of YourWebSiteName.com."

4. **My contact information:** Be clear about your contact info. Say, "Here's how the public can reach me." Clearly indicate contact information that is *not* meant to be given to the public by putting it in italics or red. Say, "Here's my private contact info for you to personally reach me...please do not include this phone number/e-mail address in the piece."

5. **Links:** If you have an online press kit, high-resolution photos that can be downloaded, or other images that might be useful, say so and make it easy for the reporter or the staff at the publication to find the material. Don't just say, "It's on my website" or "I sent it to you yesterday." Include a link in the e-mail.

After the interview, do offer to spell your name or answer any additional questions that may arise, but don't ask if you can proof or approve the written piece before it hits publication. When the piece is published, thank the reporter for the story's accuracy or for helping readers understand the topic.

Use the piece to help you improve your skills. Don't be overly judgmental or too self-critical, but pay particular attention to exactly which quotes are used and how effective they are at relaying your message. Simple, direct quotes are often preferred by writers. If you see that the article paraphrases your remarks rather than quotes you directly, it might be a sign that your messages need to be shorter, sharper, and more concise. Use every opportunity to improve your approach.

Remember your real goals. Print interviews allow you to showcase your knowledge, skills, and abilities. You simply want to educate the audience about who you are, what you do, and why that matters to them. Now that you have a published clip, leverage this—distribute the piece to everyone who might be interested.

COACHING CLINIC #14

Sometimes the best way to prepare for an interview is to imagine a finished piece as you would wish it to be. Visualize an article featuring you being dropped in an elevator and the person who picks it up is Oprah. Develop your Oprah boilerplate so you will be prepared when the chance presents itself. Boil down your information to a few clear, rich statements that are intriguing enough to make the reader want to contact you to find out more. One cool thing about print is its shelf life. A print article can end up in the hands of some very interesting people at anytime.

Have ready answers for these questions:	Brainstorm	Refine
What do you do?	Try forming an answer that starts with, "I help people by...."	
Why do people need this?	Try coming up with a response that starts with, "People come to me when they have problems with..." or "The people who are interested in what I do want me to...."	
What makes you different?	Consider framing your answer using words similar to: "The three things that I hear most often from my clients about what makes me so different are...."	
How did you get started in this field?	Try to fast-forward to the relevant part by saying, "Things really got rolling for me when...."	

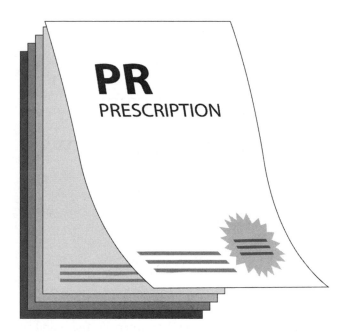

According to June Clark of Get There Media, when brainstorming, good ideas often come from surprising places:

- **Jot down even the craziest idea—don't be afraid to throw it out there and see what sticks.** No idea, no matter how seemingly crazy, should be overlooked. Let your mind go wild and write down everything you can think of. Then, put your list aside for twenty-four hours, or sleep on it. When you readdress it with a fresh eye, you'll be able to pull out what seems best. This goes for the tactics you employ, too. If you don't get the right results with one idea, it's okay to scrap it and try another.
- **If you hit a creative roadblock, do something mindless or distracting.** The best ideas/tactics/solutions usually come while taking a drive, cleaning your house, showering, or in your sleep, rather than when you're stressing over them.
- **Brainstorm with someone inventive and funny.** Two heads are often better than one. Smart, witty, and creative friends are great to call and bounce ideas off of. Even if you have a great idea, the person you share it with may offer ways to make your idea even better or simply give you a perspective you may have missed.

SESSION FIFTEEN
Broadcast Interviews

"I'm doing a radio show next week…do I call them or will they call me?"
"A talk show producer just invited me to do a TV segment—what should I wear?"

You're going to be on the radio. You have been invited to be on TV. Yea! Seize the day. Make the most out of it.

Appearing on broadcast media is often a scary proposition. Feeling relaxed and secure about what you will do before, during, and after an interview makes the process more fun. So, let's take a look at three interview stages and what you have to do to maximize the productivity of each:

- Before the interview
- During the interview
- After the interview.

Then, after we review the process, let's focus on some strategic techniques that will infuse the situation with even more promotional success.

Before the Interview

Gather the preliminary who-when-what details. Then, take care of business. Confirm the basics in writing.

For radio and TV, send a brief confirmation by e-mail. In the subject line, write: guest confirmation for (date) and (time). Keep everything simple. The e-mail should resemble a memo:

Interview Confirmation

- Host to call guest or guest to call host: If your interview is via phone, as most are, clearly state which option has been established.
- When: Interview date
- Time: Interview time

- Length: If you don't know, ask "What's the length of the planned segment?"
- What: Your name and title, such as "author of XYZ book," "creator of YourCompany.com website" and/or "president of XYZ Company."
- Guest contact info: (Your name) can be reached at (your landline phone number from where the interview will be conducted). The back-up number is (provide a cell phone or other back-up phone number).
- Where: The radio station's call letters
- Market: Coverage area
- Media contact: The name of the media contact
- Media contact number: With radio, if it's a guest-to-call-host arrangement, you need the number you are supposed to call to do the interview, and you need a backup number that you can call in case nobody answers. If the arrangement is host-to-call-guest, you will need a backup number that you can call in case they fail to call you as planned. With TV, or if you will be interviewed in the radio station's studio, you need a backup number you can call if you get lost or the front door is locked and the station's switchboard isn't answering.

Here's what else you need to ask before a TV appearance:

- "What do I need to know about parking and entering the building?" Main doors are typically locked in early hours and many studios have parking attendants or limitations on parking.
- "Do I need to be camera-ready when I arrive?" Some shows have hair or makeup stylists; many don't.
- "What time should I arrive?" Arriving thirty minutes before the interview is common.
- "Do you need any images or additional info?" Sometimes, they want a high-resolution photo of your book or product or a screen capture of your website.

Next, consider the content.

Once the logistics are squared away, focus on your message. You've got to get ready to capture the audience's attention and make a lasting impression. Realistically, you may only have two or three ten-second chunks of airtime to sum up your story. Ten seconds allows enough time for about twenty or thirty words. The trick is to make that time work for you, using strong sound bites.

A snappy sound bite is crucial. Listeners and viewers are starved for time. The competition for the audience's attention is intense. You will compete with floods, earthquakes, hurricanes, train wrecks, lying politicians, celebrity scandals, and maybe—when you least expect it—even a new panda at the zoo. Strange as it sounds, a talking head better have something really cool to say to compete with a fresh b-roll of a giant panda eating a piece of bamboo. You have to be extremely clear where you're coming from because you're only going to have an instant to explain who you are, what you do, and why it matters. Telling the audience what's in it for them usually cuts through the cacophony and captivates attention.

Keep your messages concise and memorable. Sometimes, the simplest phrase is the most profound. A carefully crafted quote can greatly improve your chances of connecting with your listeners or viewers.

In addition to grabbing the ear of the listener, your sound bites should help capture the listeners' hearts and make them care about you and what you do. To achieve this, you need to give people a reason to care.

Know what to say and say it with finesse. Create at least one line, or sound bite, that remains consistent in every interview. But, don't stick to a scripted sound bite if it feels too staged. A great sound bite stinks if trying to repeat it makes you look like you can't think on your feet. If a sound bite is unnatural or makes you sound like a parrot, it will do more harm than good. Remember, the media is interviewing you because you have information at your fingertips. You are the authority, the source. You need to know your material well enough to sound like an authority.

Relax and be authentic.

Along the lines of authenticity, make sure your wardrobe and your hairstyle are consistent with the image and the message you are trying to convey. Of course, when you are on radio, no one can see you. But for TV, choose clothing that is comfortable whether you are sitting and standing. As part of your preparation, do a dress rehearsal. Have digital photos or video taken of you wearing the clothes you will wear in the interview while you are sitting and while you are standing. Make sure your clothes look good in both positions. Knowing that you look good takes off much of the pressure when on air.

Here are some tips for looking your best on TV:

- Wear solids, not patterns. Clothing with tight patterns or pin stripes can sometimes have an optical illusion effect. Clothing with large patterns or big stripes can cause viewers to watch your clothes instead of you.
- Make sure a lavaliere or lapel microphone and transmitter can be attached to your clothing.
- If you can, find out ahead of time what the background color of the studio set will be. Take your cues from the color choices the on-air personalities are wearing. You don't want your clothing to blend into the chair or the backdrop and make you look invisible.
- Avoid flashy jewelry, especially if it jangles. Reflected light may be picked up by the camera and, if your jewelry makes noise, the sounds may be picked up by the microphone.
- Typically you will look at the host—not the camera—throughout the interview, but ask ahead of time about where to look, so that you can relax.

- Watch your hand gestures. Be aware that gestures should be small and too many gestures can be distracting on TV.

During the Interview

Focus on your passion—it will ignite your audience. Remember that the host's objectives are simply to provide timely and interesting information to the audience. Your objectives are to relay your key messages and help the media get an accurate story to the audience:

- When it's time to talk, just do it.
- Don't second guess the camera or the mic. Always act as if you are on-air.
- Avoid the temptation to explain everything you know. Do not allow yourself to go off on tangents.
- Never, ever lie.
- Don't jump to fill in silent pauses in the interview conversation. Don't worry about silence. Dead air is *their* problem.
- If you freeze for any reason, ask the reporter to repeat the question.
- If you don't have any more to say after you answer a question, stop talking.
- Every answer should make you sound good. Leave out anything negative. You want to provide great quotes and sound bites. In most cases, the host is not out to get you, even if a question seems harsh or backhanded. Be confident and direct, and frame your answers in a positive way.
- If you're asked, "Do you have anything to add?" Have something meaningful to say.

Remember your real goals. TV and radio allow you to showcase your knowledge, skills, and abilities. Your ultimate goals center around wanting to help your audience understand who you are, what you do, and why that matters to them.

After the Interview

Say thank you immediately. Then, the next day, e-mail or snail mail another thank you for the opportunity to be a guest.

What now? Leverage the TV or radio exposure to help build your brand and your reputation. Here are some too-good-to-miss tips on what to do after the media has interviewed you:

- **Get a copy.** After a piece airs, acquire clips of your interview to use for future marketing efforts. You may put together a montage of audio or video clips to show to assignment editors and segment producers. Featuring interview material will help others connect you to important opportunities that build your success. But you have to get a copy of the segment while you can. If you didn't tape it yourself, start by asking the TV station or radio station for a dub. If they can't provide one, pay for the duplication from a media monitoring service. If you need to find a media service there is a list at PRTherapy.com for you to consider.

- **Review your appearance.** The more you understand how the media works, the more you can customize the format of your message. If the whole interview wasn't used, pay special attention to which quotes were used and which ones were edited away.
- **If you like your quotes, reuse them.** Your best quotes are often formed under intense pressure. If a quote communicates your message well, use the same quote again.
- **Plan changes for next time.** With each interview, you will gain a greater understanding of the media. Are there things that you want to change before the next interview? Ask yourself the following questions:

  1. Can I fine-tune the way I talk to eliminate any undermining words, statements, or tones?
  2. Is there anything I can do to convey a more positive impression in the first seven seconds?
  3. Am I selling myself, my business, book, product or services with grace and subtlety?
  4. What can I do to improve the way I impart my message?
  5. Do I communicate confidence?
  6. Am I using my natural abilities to their fullest?
  7. Is my energy level high enough?
  8. Do I seem to have a good rapport with the on-air personality?

Master the art of bridging. You need to know how to use bridging tactics to bring the discussion back to your realm of expertise when the interviewer wanders off topic. While you must answer the person's question, your goal is to deliver your message to the audience. Bridge phrases allow you to turn the conversation back to the points you think are most important. After you have answered an off-topic question, immediately transition back to your key message.

Do this with bridge phrases like:

"What I want to emphasize is…."
"Here's the key point…."
"The part that is most important to understand is…."
"That brings up the question of…."

As you progress, you will learn easy response techniques to make rapport flow.

Move on to the next media opportunity. Make adjustments in your interview strategy and move onto the next interview. The more often you are interviewed, the better you will perform.

COACHING CLINIC #15

Writing out some sample questions with accompanying answers is a great dress rehearsal. Plus, a tightly written Q & A makes a great article to have on hand for bloggers, reporters, and even your own website or press kit.

Brainstorm Area	Sample Questions	Answers
Know the mission of your message. Below are communication goals that can be met:	Develop intriguing interview questions that you would love to be asked in each brainstorm area. In the spaces below, develop the actual questions you should be asked:	What info must be shared? In the spaces below develop the answers to the questions you should be asked:
What do you want them to ask you to help reveal who you are?		
What do you *really* wish they'd ask you to reveal more about your work?		
What questions would help you share an interesting aspect of your work?		
What could they ask that would help you discuss the importance of your product or service?		

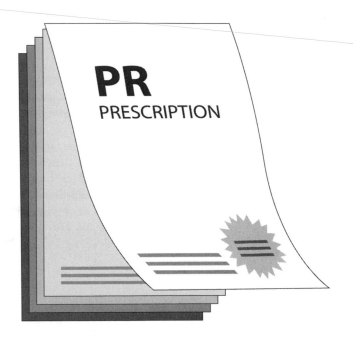

PR
PRESCRIPTION

Therese Crowley brings out the best in people. She is a broadcast host and master of the short-form broadcast interview, as well as a certified intuitive healer and performance coach (MTherese.com). Therese offers this advice:

- Before going on the air, take a silent moment: Pause, breathe (very important—calms nerves and lowers the vocal pitch), and silently ask that the right words be put in your mouth.
- Remember: It's not about you. It's about your message. It's not about what you're here to get out of this appearance, it's the message you're here to bring. No need to worry how you look or sound; you will be perfect when you focus on the message.
- Broadcasters are like other human beings; we are susceptible to flattery. When you are stumped by a question, respond, heartily, "That is an excellent question." It buys you time to think, and it gives the host a warm feeling about you for recognizing his "excellent" question.
- Time is ticking. Get in and out quickly, with grace. Be easy. "A pleasure to be here." "Thanks for having me." "Good to be with you."
- So very few people write a thank-you note. Follow up with a brief thanks (not too effusive) and the host will remember you fondly, and think to call you again. You now have a friend and ally on the air.

SESSION SIXTEEN
Live Bookings

"I just got a written invitation to be on a panel at a prestigious conference six months from tomorrow. Two whole pages describe where to park and how to find the stage, but there's only one cryptic line about the topic. I'm terrified. What do I do?"

It's true that in a world full of communicators, even the most confident people experience a fleeting moment when they sincerely believe they'd rather die than stand behind a microphone, in front of a classroom, or on the stage of a major auditorium. In fact, surveys and opinion polls consistently indicate that public speaking is often feared more than death.

What's behind those feelings of fear?

Usually, it's about not knowing what to expect, being uncertain about what is required, and sensing that the event is doomed to end in failure.

If these thoughts are running through your head when you think of public speaking, you're not alone. In fact, welcome to the club. Feelings of fear and anxiety are likely to creep in at key moments along the live-event trail. But, as pesky as these feelings are, they can be useful and manageable if you address them.

Let's review some key moments to help transport you successfully through the following stages:

- Before the event day
- At the door
- On stage
- Right after your appearance
- The day after.

Then, after we hit the high spots, we'll focus on some techniques that will inject even more promotional success into the situation.

Before the Event Day

Focus on your topic. Decide what you're going to talk about and do the work it takes to wow 'em.

Don't try to tell everything you know about your topic. And, unless you're an author who was specifically invited to read a passage from your own book, don't plan to read to your audience. You are there to talk, not to read from notes.

Set aside enough time to really prepare for whatever you are going to talk about or say. If you're hell-bent on delivering a pithy, crisp, memorable message, get hell-bent on preparing for it. Give yourself enough time to do what it takes. Schedule prep time on your calendar the same way you would schedule any other event. Devote every minute you need to pull it off.

It sometimes takes a while to find your authentic voice as a speaker. Take the time to listen to how you talk on the telephone, with strangers on an airplane, with people in the grocery store line—it is often these times that your real personality comes through. Don't leave your real personality behind when you're standing in front of an audience.

Don't forget about the audience, either. Consider who the audience is and what their expectations may be. Ask yourself the following questions:

- Is my content geared toward Newbies or Hardcores or a mix of both?
- What level of detail and complexity is appropriate for this group?
- What do they already know about my subject?
- What parts interest this audience most and why?
- What do they hope my presentation will achieve for them?
- How will what I share with them help them?

Plan to tell a tale. When people are in the room with you, they like hearing a story that makes them feel connected to you. Give them what they want. Take a fresh look at your personal experiences and develop some fun or interesting anecdotes that illustrate your main talking points.

After you get an initial grip on it all, talk to the host. Once you've collected your ideas and have decided your basic direction about topic and content, it is time to get some feedback on some of the logistics.

You may feel reluctant to bother the host. You may wonder if you will look needy or unprepared, or perhaps come across as jittery. This is a possibility if you approach the situation like you're doing something wrong or offer too much information about your personal fears or character flaws.

Simply call and say, "I know how important it is to keep communication lines open. I'm calling to go over some key details with you so that we're both ready for the upcoming event."

Here are some questions for you to ask:

What about handouts? Do they want handouts? (Do you have any?) If they would like them, find out how many handouts you need to bring so that every member of the audience gets one. Or, will the host duplicate them for you? Understand that if they duplicate them for you, you cannot control the quality of the print job.

If you use handouts, make sure your contact information and website address are on every one. If appropriate, refer your audience to a specially designed page on your website for access to more material. This will drive traffic to your website and help you achieve repeat visitors.

How about audio-visuals? Discuss any audio-visual needs or expectations. Do you need any of the following?

- Screen
- Lectern
- Light pointer
- Lavaliere microphone (also known as a necklace, lapel or pendant mic)
- Qualified projectionist
- Slide projector
- Public address system
- Room that can be darkened for screen presentations
- Special film projector
- Flip chart with easel
- Display easel
- Additional microphones for a panel of guests
- Laptop for use with LCD projectors
- Internet connection.

Who will introduce me? Offer to send a copy of your introduction directly to the person who will introduce you. When you prepare your introduction, keep the script conversational and keep it short. If you give too much information, you run the risk of the presenter editing it down to focus on points that you never imagined important or reading every line word-for-word and making you feel like you just previewed your own eulogy.

What's the venue look like? Talk about special room set-up options. Do you have a preference for the way things are arranged?

- Do you need a head table?
- Want a podium?
- How about a circle of chairs?
- Do you need the room arranged classroom style, offering tables for participants to write on?
- Do you prefer theatre-style seating?
- How about a back-of-room display table?

What's the back-of-the-room policy? Will you be provided with display space to sell products at the back of the room of your live event? If so, what is the best way for products to get to the venue? What support will be available during and after the event? How will sales transactions be handled? Will cash, checks, or credit cards be accepted? Who will be the person handling the transactions?

You may want to bring an assistant to handle sales or ask that the hosting organization provide one and then meet with this person before your presentation.

Will the event be taped? Recognize your intellectual property rights. Seek clarity about a host's intentions for recording the live event. Find out if your appearance will be taped, filmed, or otherwise recorded. If so, find out if your appearance will be broadcast on radio, TV, or on the Internet, or packaged as a video or audio recording for distribution or sale.

What is the budget? Money is a sticky subject, but you need to know how things will be handled.

- **Will you be paid to appear?** If so, you need to be know how much to charge. If you don't know what to charge, find out what is reasonable in your field for your level of experience. Also, consider what is reasonable for an organization to pay. If you are not sure about your fees, try this: When they ask, "What is your rate?", answer, "I'm sure we can work something out. What is your budget range?"
- **Is there an honorarium?** Sometimes a payment is given as a gift to the speaker. Depending on the size and affluence of the group, this honorarium could be enough to buy a drink or enough to buy a memorable dinner for everyone in your party.
- **What about expenses?** The host of your event may cover your expenses or you may be expected to cover your own expenses. Expenses are typically a separate entity from both fees and honorariums. Expenses might include airfare, taxi-fare, car rental costs, lodging, but never anything of a personal nature. That means the new outfit you buy for the event does not qualify as an expense a host would typically agree to pay.

Get it in writing. Once you've hammered out the details, make sure those details are put into writing to assure clarity and eliminate misunderstandings. The only way you may ever get details in writing from some groups is to write down the details yourself.

If you prepare the paperwork, approach the host with something like this: "Thanks for the productive meeting! Below, are the key points from our conversation. If you understood any detail differently, please let me know this week so we can clarify. Next Monday I will share our details with my office so we can move things forward here." Set a deadline like "this week" or "next Monday" so that ample time is given and closure can occur.

Phrase your communication so that the underlying idea is clear: "This is how it is, unless you speak up now." Of course, such a ploy amounts to little more than a gentleman's handshake. It's certainly no binding contract, but it is better than nothing. If you want a binding contract, require a binding contract.

At the Door

Smile. On event day, walk in like you own the place even if you feel like crawling under the nearest table to puke. Look people in the eye, nod, smile, and be likeable. Do not behave as if you're wired on caffeine.

Show no fear. Realize that being afraid is one thing but *looking* afraid is something you can control. Looking afraid puts everyone else under stress and can make the whole environment uncomfortable. Looking *un*afraid helps you, your hosts, and your audience get off on the right foot together.

Never tell anyone at the event, including the audience, how nervous you are. They don't want to know. Don't tell them nonverbally either. Do not shuffle your feet, chew on your fingernails, or wring your hands incessantly.

With practice, manifestations of fear can be stopped. Good strategies include:

• Take a few deep breaths and exhale slowly.
• Remind yourself that you are the knowledgeable one.
• Smile and nod at one or two members of the audience. This makes them your companions in this and you can then speak as if you are simply addressing them.

Treat all the people who are at the event the same way you would treat new friends. Smile at them. Be friendly, spontaneous, and, most importantly, be yourself.

Locate the players. Find out who will introduce you and make sure that person has a copy of the introduction you have prepared. Bring a copy of the introduction with you; sometimes original plans have changed by event day and the person who was going to introduce you may have failed to pass on his copy to the person who now is going to introduce you. If you like questions raised throughout your talk or held until the end, let this person know. He can instruct the audience appropriately during the introduction.

If you have a PowerPoint or a video, make quick friends with the person who will serve as your visual aids operator.

The event facilitator is usually a good person to ask how and when the room will be called to order.

On Stage

Focus on your passion—it will ignite your audience. When it's time to talk, just do it. Keep in mind that you really can control most of the individual factors that comprise how the audience perceives you. In fact, knowing what the components typically are can help you be a better speaker right from the get-go.

If your audience kept a scorecard, they'd mark you up or down on a dozen factors:

1. **Your Big Opener**
   - Break the ice in a memorable way that's natural for you.
   - Say who you are and why you are sharing your information.
   - Tell them what you plan to do.
2. **Your Volume**
   - Talk loud enough to be heard. Make sure the audience can hear you clearly throughout the room.
3. **Your Pace**
   - Don't sound like you are in a big hurry.
   - Is your flow of ideas too fast or too slow?
4. **Your Knowledge**
   - Remember your goal is to help people glimpse behind the curtain of your world and see how you do things or what you know.
   - Do you seem comfortable with your material?
5. **Your Energy Level**
   - Do you seem enthusiastic?
   - Are you about to have a Tom-Cruise-on-Oprah's-couch moment?
6. **Your Eyes Have It**
   - Are you making eye contact across the audience?
   - Don't be a note-bound reader.
7. **Your Body Language**
   - Is your posture straight and confident?
   - Do your hand gestures enhance what you are saying?
8. **Your WIFM Rating**
   - "What's In It for Me?" Tell them what's in it for them—they want to know. In fact, they want to unmistakably know what to be excited about. Be very clear about it.
9. **Your Flow of Info**
   - Attention to structure in the preparation stage pays off in the delivery stage.
   - Is the order of information logical and easy to follow?
   - Is your content relevant, interesting, and engaging?
10. **Your Use of Visuals**
    - Have more than one copy of your PowerPoint presentation. Save it on a CD, a flash drive, and the desktop of your laptop. Technology isn't foolproof, so be ready to go on with the show if there's a glitch. Don't ever put yourself in a position where you must rely on PowerPoint to speak.
    - If you're using PowerPoint, know how to move forward and backward through the slides without becoming lost or confused.

- Are your visual aids easy to read? Less is definitely more on stage. No single slide or individual flip chart page should have more than ten to twelve words.
- Do your visuals effectively support what you're talking about? Do you use them adeptly?
- If you plan to have a live connection to the Internet, be prepared for a glitch. You could have screen captures printed on paper as a backup or you could use prepared slides of Internet pages as a backup.

11. **Your Water Cooler Appeal**
    - As mentioned earlier, the people in the room want to hear a story that makes them feel connected to you. Develop some anecdotes that illustrate your main talking points.
    - Tell them a story that they want to repeat to the gang.

12. **Your Big Closer**
    - If you're taking questions from the audience, stop your Q&A session to allow five to ten minutes so you can end with prepared comments on a completely controlled note.
    - Quit when it's time to quit.

Right after Your Appearance

Smile again at everyone.

A rule to remember is no negative remarks onsite. None. You don't complain, whine, or diss. Never a frown, a scowl, or a rolling of your eyes.

You may be dying to compare notes with the friend who came with you to the event. You may be ready to trade insights with the host. You may even think it's safe to crawl into a bathroom stall and call home.

Don't.

Someone will overhear and rat you out.

The Day After

Formally express thanks. Drop a note, call, or e-mail to say you appreciated the opportunity.

Now Let's Ratchet It Up.

Once you move past the *I'll-die-on-stage* mode to the *I-am-dying-to-get-back-on-stage* mode, it's time to take it up a few notches. What can you do or bring to the next event to get more return for the effort?

Here are some too-good-to-miss opportunities: Before the event, help event planners promote your appearance in a way that will help you connect with your audience. Find out early-on what kind of deadlines they may have for promotions.

- Ask if you will be mentioned in a newsletter or on a website.
- Ask what kinds of deadlines you need to meet and what kind of material you need to provide.
- Ask if they need a digital picture or image.
- Ask if they'd like your bio or a description of your talk.
- Ask if the media will be invited.

Promote your session! Getting people interested in your session is more than just coming up with the title and showing up. If you have a blog, write about it—tell people you're speaking. And make the most of the opportunity. Secure invitations to be a guest on TV or radio by alerting local media of your event and your availability to be interviewed.

Bring a sign-up sheet. The sign-up sheet should have space for attendees to write their e-mail address and their name. What are they signing up for? Could be your newsletter, a special tip sheet, a recap of the meeting, or a list of your favorite resources. The idea is to begin building a relationship.

Ask for business cards. And, hand out business cards, too. In fact, if it's appropriate, make the process fun by allowing attendees to drop cards in a bowl for a chance to win some kind of prize, such as a report you normally charge for or a thirty-minute phone consultation.

Take photos. Your events don't become real to the rest of the world until you come back with pictures. When it comes to event photography, you want action pictures that tell the story, share the excitement of the moment, and help illustrate possibilities for similar success at future venues.

How do you achieve this if all you have is a snapshot camera and the help of a tag-along family member or a just-assigned, never-met-you-before event volunteer?

It's *not* impossible.

The most important steps are aiming the camera and clicking the shutter button. Put the designated appointed photographer at ease by telling her you feel success is achieved merely by the aiming and shooting of the camera. Mean it. Then, clarify how many shots are available to take and how many you want taken during the event. You want as many shots as possible without running out of digital space or film. You can cull out the bad ones later.

Here's an assignment checklist for you to give directly to your paparazzi person:

1. Get a photo of me in a few poses with the event signage visible, like the newspaper does at those weekly chamber of commerce events.
2. Get me in some candid shots, speaking to the group. It's fine, even preferable, to frame the shots so that it includes the backs or sides of heads in the audience. Try to make it evident that there really are people attending my event and listening to my talk.

3. Get me in some casual one-on-one shots. Capture the meaningful chat between me and someone in the group. Zoom in so you can see the interaction.
4. Get a couple of candid shots of the faces of the group in general.
5. Get some pictures that feature me as seen from the back of the line of the people waiting to talk to me.

Remember, point-and-click are the most important steps. Take lots of photos to increase the chances of one or two turning out to be decent. Sounds obvious, but it's often forgotten that two untrained people armed with cameras can get a better variety of images than one untrained person. But, beware: Three untrained photographers will turn into a Three Stooges routine faster than you can poke Curly's eyes out.

What about the camera itself? Cool cameras are only cool if you know how to use them. Don't be afraid of inexpensive equipment for amateur photographers. A disposable camera can be better than a sophisticated one if the sophisticated one is too intimidating for the person using it. Plus, a cheap camera is less likely to be lost, damaged, or stolen, especially if you perma-marker your name and phone number on it. Make sure camera batteries are fresh. If it's digital, make sure the memory card is empty. If it's a film camera, make sure the film is correctly loaded. No one wants to be the one to change the batteries or replace the film at the event. No camera? If you get there and realize you forgot the camera, get a few images from a cell phone's camera—an image is worth a thousand words and can give Twitter pals something to tweet about.

- When you hold your book or product, don't morph into a classic Vanna White pose, but do make the item casually visible.
- Be aware of empty front rows. Graciously ask an event person to help people fill the front and center seats. In event photos, empty front rows look like no one came, even if the room is packed.

Consider video. If you can capture your live presentation on video, go for it. Later, you can choose a clip from the footage for inclusion in the promotional video collage we've talked about or to place on YouTube or your website.

COACHING CLINIC #16

Here's a guided brainstorming activity that can help you craft and set the pace for the beginning, middle, and end of any talk.

The Opening	Tell them what you plan to do:
Figure on allotting about 20 percent of your talk time to your opening segment.	• Break the ice in some memorable way. • Say who you are and why you are sharing your information. • Quickly explain what the presentation is about and what you will be covering. • Tell them what's in it for them.

The Middle Ground	Do what you promised to do:
Figure on allotting about 50 percent of your talk time covering the middle ground.	• Grab their attention with a story or provide a pithy quote. • Give details of your topic in a logical order. • Use real stories to illustrate your points. • Tell them how this information applies to them.

The Closer	Tell them what you just covered:
Figure on allotting 30 percent of your talk time wrapping things up for the closer.	• Recap the high spots of your main points. • Explain exactly how your information should be used to help them. • Give them the next to-do steps. • Ask them to ask questions. • Encourage them to stay in touch with you. • Quit talking when you're done.

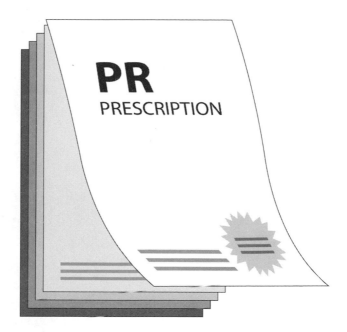

Dan Collins is the senior director of media relations for Mercy Medical Center in Baltimore. He lectures to undergrads at Loyola College, where he teaches an "Introduction to Public Relations" course. Dan offers this advice:

I studied "Contact Speaking" with a Jesuit instructor who, the first day of the class, announced he was going to teach us all we needed to know in the first five minutes of the period.

He then proceeded to scrawl the letters "S," "L," "U," and "P" on the blackboard. SLUP, we learned, was an acronym for:

- **Slow:** You have to speak slowly so that everyone can clearly understand you.
- **Loud:** Can the folks in the back row hear you as well as those down front?
- **Upright:** Avoid swaying like a metronome, or people will be concentrating on your swaying and not on what you're saying.
- **Poised:** That is, don't panic. The best example of this comes from the 1984 Olympics when, before a crowd of 100,000, not to mention the millions watching on TV, an athlete ran into the Los Angeles Coliseum to light the Olympic flame, began to give a speech—and froze. Couldn't remember what he was to say next. Talk about public speaking pressure. So what did he do? He repeated the part he remembered. And then the memory chain kicked in, the rest came to him, and he finished his speech. That is poise.

Of course, these letters also spell PLUS, but Fr. Donaho, the instructor, thought SLUP was a funny sounding word and therefore we'd be more apt to remember it. That was twenty-eight years ago, and I still remember Slow, Loud, Upright, and Poised.

PHASE VI

Building on Your Success

When I began my career, I was the *other* newswriter at a tiny radio station in the northern end of Los Angeles County. I was the one with the ponytail, the youngest employee in the building. Our station was behind a Jack In The Box fast food restaurant, where at that time I could have made more money as cashier than I would ever make in radio. But, lucky for me, I followed my passion.

I loved radio, loved to interview local leaders, and loved to hear my stories hit the air.

When the station decided to launch a talk show, I was really excited. I greeted the new host each morning when he crept into the building with red eyes, the same wrinkled shirt, and a sour expression on his weathered face. One day, soon after his arrival, the Big Boss told me, "Hey, we'll let you be his talk show producer if you think you are able to get a big name to come on his show. Can you get a big name?"

I was so thrilled, my heart pounded. "You bet, I will."

And I did. I got Mike Wallace, and most of the congressmen across the country, Hollywood producers, some comic geniuses like Bob Hope, some newcomers like Jeff Foxworthy, aerospace legends like Chuck Yeager, and astronauts and test pilots, and even the vice president of the United States.

And, along the way, that surly talk show host turned out to be very talented, bright, and funny. He was ready to run in any direction I dared to dream and he soon became a lifelong friend.

We set up literacy programs with schools and invited authors as radio guests, and pretty soon the largest New York publishers were calling to offer us interviews with folks like Madeleine L'Engle and Dom DeLuise. I personally had the time of my life.

The big "wow" moment came a few years later when I found out two things. First, everyone else at the station had been afraid of the surly host and, when he blindly made the recommendation for me to be his producer, it was largely because I was the only one in the building who bothered to greet him.

But perhaps more surprising still was the other discovery: The Big Boss had requested big name guests, but my snagging the vice president of the United States was not who he had in mind. The only big name that the Big Boss really hoped I would book was the mayor of our little town.

I'd booked the mayor as a regular guest—beyond him, I'd overshot expectations, and nobody said a word. I still think, "Wow, isn't it absolutely amazing what a person with an imagination can do when fear isn't a blocking factor, a general direction is identified, and you're so excited about what you're doing that you just keep moving?"

Actually, it's more than amazing. And, year after year, I've been most fortunate to accompany client after client on their own unique journeys. Now, it's your turn. So, get up, get moving, and follow your heart. Just imagine where your passion will take you, and if you can't imagine it, well, I bet I can.

Make Your Past Work for You

Not many first-time novelists get written up in USA Today. But sometimes the combination of the author's real life and his novel's fiction is too good to be overlooked. Case in point: Chris Edwards.

Fresh out of college, Chris, a card-carrying member of Mensa with professional experience riding bulls in the rodeo circuit, wrote a debut novel called Angel on the Lost Highway. He, like all first-time authors, dreamed of making a huge promotional splash, but he soon realized that the pool of reporters willing to read a first novel was nearly dry.

Instead of giving up, Chris decided he should share more details about himself the next time he sent out a press release. His next release not only detailed his novel but also his personal background. Voila! A reporter from USA Today called him.

The journalist recognized that there was indeed a story to be told, but the real story was not about an author's intriguing book; it was about the book's intriguing author. The article that ran in USA Today told a quirky inspirational tale about a smart, young writer who had survived riding bulls professionally long enough to write an entertaining novel set in the rodeo world.

PR Tip: Don't forget to maximize your relevant past experiences when you talk about your current work.

SESSION SEVENTEEN
Getting Real—Making Promotions Authentic

"How do I gain control in a bigger way? How do I tie it all together?"

No matter if you're promoting your own products or services, building a creative career, or leading a heartfelt cause in the nonprofit world, PR results begin to markedly improve when you make a deliberate decision to take an authentic approach to publicity.

"Authentic" simply means that at every turn in the pursuit of publicity you have to remain real with yourself and with the world.

Be true to who *you* are.

Find and focus on the real truth that needs to be shared with your audience. Your work—your products and services—is nothing less than a tangible expression of who you are and what you care about. You've been asked this before, but it helps to think about it again…and again:

- Who are you?
- What do you care about?
- What group of people are you trying to help?
- How are you making a true difference in the lives of others?

Until now, you may have never considered looking deeply at your products and services in regards to what they really say about who you are. However, your work is your fingerprint in the world. It's that unique, that important, that relevant, and that connected to your own personal identity. Your work is an embodiment of your passion. The more passionate you are, the better your work will be. By now, you have a real sense that your products and services, and yourself, all fit together in the promotional game.

You Need a Platform!

To that end, when you believe in what you're doing, you absolutely must do what it takes to reach the people who need your products and services. The easiest and most reliable way to get and keep getting authentic publicity for your products and services (and for yourself) is to build a platform. The truth is in this Field of Dreams, if you build a strong and steady platform, publicity will come, and, with it, the means for sustainable success.

So, what exactly is a platform?

In the publishing world and other arenas, your platform encompasses how well your name is known and your work is recognized. For writers—as well as entrepreneurs, artists, designers, and others—the stature of your platform is universally measured by what you can bring to the table in terms of promotion.

Imagine a three-legged table.

To help you wrap your brain around the concept, try this: Metaphorically, your platform is a three-legged table. In this perspective, it's not about what you can bring to the table; your platform *is* the table. You can create and sustain success if you know how it should be constructed:

- One leg is all about effectively running your promotional outreach.
- One leg is all about managing your resources.
- One leg is all about constantly developing the core talent and skill to produce the best services or products you can.

Since each of these three table legs represents a core area of your platform, you need each leg to be long enough to function properly in order for your platform to be successful. One great leg cannot compensate endlessly for the other two. The best promotions in the world cannot incessantly overcome poor products or services. The best products and services can not continuously overcome poor promotions. And on it goes.

Every table leg needs to bear its share of the weight. The most common problem associated with building a platform is that people figuratively build their platforms using table legs of three very different lengths. One leg is typically very long and well-developed, one leg is quite short and under-achieving, and one entire leg is sometimes missing altogether. When the three table legs of your platform are forced to operate at uneven lengths, it will feel like your success is teetering and wobbling—that your business life is unbalanced, uncertain, fragile, and out-of-kilter.

Put an end to topsy-turvy, out-of-control feelings. As you learn to level out the structural legs of your platform so that each area can function better, feelings of uncertainty will be replaced by feelings of stability. Your guidance from the gut instincts will become more visceral and trustworthy. Promotional opportunities will become better in both quality and abundance. As a result, your platform will command attention in your industry and, by having a steady table of your own making, you'll have more to bring to any table you choose. You will discover that building your platform is actually completely quantifiable and doable.

Sound impossible? It isn't.

First, examine your promotions leg.

For the promotional leg of your platform, your big goal is to reach out to every individual in your target market, presenting reasons they need your products or services. Even the tiniest grassroots-style motion in your promotional arena can be transformed into something extraordinary if the other legs of your platform are functional. If the other areas are not working, you'll wonder why even exceptional PR achievements are not impacting your bottom line.

It's critical to understand how the three areas work in tandem with each other.

So, take a closer look at the other two legs of your platform. You may be surprised and relieved to realize that three platform legs working at entry-level ability can produce more results than some über-sophisticated PR machine stuck working with two platform legs that are nonoperational or barely running. The truth is that steadily working to get simple basics into place can actually launch you toward a higher level of success than you ever imagined achievable.

Next, examine your resource management leg.

Your resource management leg will dramatically enhance or curtail the scope of your promotional efforts. When you hear the term "resource," you may think this area is all about money. The good news is that money isn't the only resource you have or need. And, the even better news is that you're wealthy enough right now, with the resources you can currently access, to get where you want to be, if you will do what it takes to make the resource leg of your platform operational.

How?

Take a closer look. The resource leg of your platform is actually comprised of three dovetailed parts:

- Money
- Time
- People.

Money. Money is a tough subject for everybody. You either have it, or you don't. You either want it, or you don't know what to do with it. You either think it holds great advantages, or you suspect it's the root of all evil.

It helps to know that your personal worth and your bank account's value are two very different items. Don't confuse the two. Money is simply great, but great is not simply money. Money is just one of the three resources in which good management is important. If you have money, you can make it work for you. If you don't have money, you can leverage other resources that you do have to compensate for the lack of money you think you need.

Projections and budgets are an important part of managing this resource. Take the time to make them, both on an annual basis and on a project basis.

Time. Time is tricky. You routinely have plenty or not enough of it. It either races by or drags its sorry butt. The cool thing about time is that the playing field is level. From peasants to presidents, you, like everyone else, get twenty-four hours each day. You, like everyone else, get twelve months each year.

In spite of how it may seem, you ultimately can do what you want with your time. You can invest it or waste it on activities or with people of your choice.

Remember, time is another major resource that belongs to you and needs to be managed. If you don't have enough money to get what you need, you can usually find a way to trade time for what you want and must have.

People. Your people pool is measured by how many people you know and how many people know you. You, like everyone else, have a world full of possibilities. It's commonly said that it's not what you know, it's who you know. So start shaking some hands. Get to know whom you need to know. Remember, people are the most important part of life. Everyone has a lesson to share with you. Everyone has a gift to offer. And don't be a stingy gut, because it's not all about what you can get; it's about what you can give, too. Be someone who has something to offer. Be the kind of person others feel they need to know. You can cultivate who you are and will become.

You can become more successful promotionally and on every other level when you fully understand the nature of your wealth. Money. Time. People. All of your valuable resources require careful cultivation, development, and management. That means you need to make money and allocate money wisely. Spend time and invest time intelligently. Cultivate relationships sensibly.

It is often a startling relief to discover that by simply doing the basic fundamentals of good resource management, you will shore up and secure this crucial leg of your platform and all of your framework will benefit from it.

Finally, examine your talent and skill leg.

All of your promotional efforts are directly connected to the talent and skill leg of your platform—without this leg, you'd have nothing to promote. In this area of your platform, your biggest goal is to produce tangible evidence of your talent and skill. It isn't enough to simply develop talent *or* skill. You must develop both together. The right balance of talent and skill—and a bit of hard work—will create a product or service worth promoting.

Focus on your talent. Talent is widely understood as the something special, the creative spark, the electric energy that a person has. It is fueled by passion. Doing what you love transforms your talent from a delicate flicker to an inextinguishable fire.

Talent is a gift.

You've seen talent most clearly in certain outstanding people. Many share the gift of bringing ideas to life through spoken words: Martin Luther King and Eleanor Roosevelt are two examples. Many share the gift of turning sounds into music: think of Mozart and Carole King. Many share a talent for calling attention to the funny side of a given situation: Bob Hope, Ellen DeGeneres, and Bill Cosby all come to mind.

Many share a gift of transforming a blank canvass or blank page into a gripping and memorable experience: Matisse, Van Gogh, Ernest Hemingway, and Stephen King are examples.

Like these talented people, you have your own unique talent. Your talent is linked to what you love to do. But talent alone isn't enough. Development of talent requires development of skill.

Focus on your skill. Talent and skill develop in a sequential fashion—you must first develop some basic skills before you can develop some higher-level talents. Each new skill that you acquire builds on the last skill developed. As skills are learned, talent levels naturally and instinctively grow. Skill helps natural talent become stronger.

Skills include using the tools of your trade. Learning to read music is a skill that helps one's natural talent for music grow. The mechanics of good grammar is a learned skill that sets free the talent for storytelling. Mixing colors is a skill that painters need to facilitate their talent for art.

You may acquire the skills of a master in your chosen field and be quite talented; however, having high levels of skill and talent and doing something with them are two different things.

For this leg of your platform to be operational, you must use your talent and skill to develop finished products and services that can be packaged for the marketplace.

Focus on producing tangible results. A half-finished novel doesn't cut it. A half-painted canvas won't make the grade. A bright idea for an innovative new business isn't enough. You must create products or services—from start to finish.

Don't just brainstorm the big idea. Don't just immerse yourself in the dreamy-start part, focusing on all the incredible, intricate plans. Do the whole thing.

At some level, in some capacity, finish one of the things you've started. Find a stopping point that makes one part of what you do transform into a finished product or service. Package something completely and wholly.

As your talent and skill work to produce tangible products and services, this leg of your platform will develop and grow. Building a steady platform is the easiest and most reliable way to acquire and sustain authentic publicity for your products and services—and for yourself. The stronger and better this leg becomes, the stronger and better the entire platform becomes.

So, how does your platform stack up?

In most cases, you will find that the shorter table legs, the areas with the most gap, are the legs geared to promotions or resources. The longest leg is most often the one geared toward the development of the talent and skill that produced your product or service. But, that is not always how it plays out. Sometimes your personal or professional experiences will expedite growth in promotions or resources and actually be the defining factor that reveals your talent or skill. The important thing is to realistically work with what you've got, whatever it is.

COACHING CLINIC #17

How do you assess your own three platform legs and actually go about the process to plan, build, and define success for your endeavors?

Here's where you'll likely have a real "aha" moment about what your platform is and what it can become. Start by taking an objective look at where things stand and how out-of-kilter they may actually be. Look closely at the way the various elements of the legs of your platform actually stack up.

Take the following assessment test to measure the legs of your platform. To expedite needed growth, consider ways to turn items you mark NO into items you can mark YES. Get ready to do what it takes to make the changes you need.

Promotions Leg
1. Y/N   Do you have a database of promotional contacts?
2. Y/N   Do you have a press kit?
3. Y/N   Do you have a website?
4. Y/N   Do you have a press release?
5. Y/N   Do you have a business card?
6. Y/N   Do you have a promotional postcard?
7. Y/N   Do you have a basic advertisement for your product or service?
8. Y/N   Do you have a written description of your product/service?
9. Y/N   Do you have a bio/profile?
10. Y/N   Do you have a publicity picture of yourself?
11. Y/N   Do you have a publicity photo of your product or any samples, copies, or photos of your actual work?
12. Y/N   Do you have a brochure or flyer describing what you do?
13. Y/N   Do you have a wish list for where you want publicity hits?
14. Y/N   Do you have electronic versions of your promotional materials?
15. Y/N   Do you have a phone script for the cold calls you need to make?
16. Y/N   Do you have a strong voice-mail message for people to hear?
17. Y/N   Do you have formal letterhead?
18. Y/N   Do you have a brief, but written, promotional plan?
19. Y/N   Do you have any awards?

20. Y/N Does another organization have awards that were acquired with your participation?
21. Y/N Do you have letters or memos expressing gratitude for your personal or professional achievements?
22. Y/N Do you have newspaper clippings that highlight your activities?
23. Y/N Do you have photographs that illustrate your work or your involvement in key activities?
24. Y/N Do you have radio interview experience? Do you have MP3s of the interviews?
25. Y/N Do you have TV interview experience? Do you have digital files or DVDs of your appearances?
26. Y/N Do you appear on multiple websites when your name is Googled?

Good for you! Add up all the Yes answers. How many are there? Now, imagine the promotions leg of your three-legged table as being divided into 26 equal segments (one for each question above): In your mind, color in each segment you answered Yes to, starting from the top and working your way down. How long is the leg? What can you do to make it longer (which NOs can be turned into YES)?

Resource Management Leg

1. Y/N Do you use a planning calendar, Blackberry, or PDA for appointments?
2. Y/N Do you have written objectives for goals?
3. Y/N Do you have a schedule reminding you of recurring tasks?
4. Y/N Do you schedule follow-up tasks on a calendar or on a list?
5. Y/N Do you block out personal time?
6. Y/N Do you block out down time?
7. Y/N Do you have a rate card?
8. Y/N Do you have a budget for projected expenses?
9. Y/N Do you have set goals for projected income?
10. Y/N Do you have a basic contract for your services?
11. Y/N Do you have a basic price list for your products?
12. Y/N Do you have a set hourly rate?
13. Y/N Do you know the cost of competing products or services?
14. Y/N Do you have an invoice form to send to customers?
15. Y/N Do you have a bookkeeping system?
16. Y/N Do you follow up with your buyers to alert them to other buying opportunities?
17. Y/N Do you have a list of people who have bought your products or services?
18. Y/N Do you have a coach or a mentor?
19. Y/N Do you provide mentoring for others?

20. Y/N   Do you have a group of confidantes?
21. Y/N   Do you have a list of networking opportunities or a formal list of people you want to meet?
22. Y/N   Do you have the help you actually need: an assistant, manager, agent, publicist, or other person to share the work load?
23. Y/N   Do you have an easy-to-access database of your personal contacts?
24. Y/N   Do you have an easy e-mail address for people to contact you?
25. Y/N   Do you have an easy-to-use database of media contacts?
26. Y/N   Do you update your databases routinely?

Great work! Add up all the Yes answers. How many did you get this time? Once again, imagine your table, this time focusing on the resource management leg; color in a segment of the leg for each question where your answer was Yes. Is this leg longer of shorter than the promotions leg? Which NOs can be turned into YES?

Talent and Skill Leg

1. Y/N   Can you tell others what your top three natural talents are?
2. Y/N   Do people remark upon your special abilities?
3. Y/N   Do you know what level of development your talent has reached?
4. Y/N   Do you have a written summary of your skills?
5. Y/N   Do you have a resume?
6. Y/N   Are you actively learning ways to improve your skills?
7. Y/N   Can you teach your skills to others?
8. Y/N   Do you have unfinished projects that will eventually become products or services?
9. Y/N   Do you have one or more finished products or specific services?
10. Y/N   Do you have three or more finished products?
11. Y/N   Do you have three or more services that you can offer now?
12. Y/N   Are your products and services packaged clearly enough for other people to help you sell them?
13. Y/N   Do you give back to the community by sharing your talents and skills?
14. Y/N   Can you clearly communicate information in both verbal and written formats as appropriate for the needs of your target audience?
15. Y/N   Do you believe in your own ideas?
16. Y/N   Do you listen carefully and manage information efficiently?
17. Y/N   Do you know what you do best and farm out the rest of the necessary work to a network of partners or vendors?
18. Y/N   Do you trust your own instincts?
19. Y/N   Do you know how fast you can work and can you accurately estimate how long a proposed project will take you to complete?

20. Y/N   Are you keeping pace with new technologies in your field. Are you actively aware of emerging and developing changes/interventions in the way people think and leverage technology for your field?

21. Y/N   Do people who know you well believe that you have a powerful positive attitude?

22. Y/N   Are you able to vary or adjust your personal approach or style according to situational demands?

23. Y/N   Are you able to deal with change?

24. Y/N   Are you able to sustain a sense of humor under pressure?

25. Y/N   Do you develop a rapport with others and form working relationships?

26. Y/N   Do you have leadership experience? Can you supervise, direct and motivate others to achieve a recognized objective?

Excellent work! How many questions did you answer Yes to? As before, color that many segments in the talent and skill leg on your imaginary three-legged table. How does this leg compare to the other two? If you want to make the talent and skill leg grow longer, you need to figure out what you must do to make each item marked NO turn into a YES.

Assess yourself

How did you do? Which leg is the shortest? That leg needs the most attention right away. Think about these results as you continue to build your strategy in the next chapter.

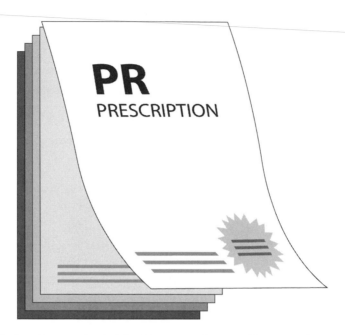

Gail F. Goodman is the CEO of Constant Contact (ConstantContact.com), a company that helps with e-mail marketing and online surveying. She knows the value of staying in touch with your audience:

- **Stay connected to your customers.** Know what they want and how they want you to communicate with them. Connect with them using cost-effective and personalized methods. E-mail marketing is one tool that can help you build stronger relationships with your customers and result in big cost savings.
- **Share your expertise.** People want to learn from you. The exchange of knowledge turns trust into loyalty. E-mail marketing campaigns can feature your knowledge and serve as an ongoing resource for your customers. Inspire repeat business by putting your value, expertise, and brand clearly out in front.

SESSION EIGHTEEN
Your Self-Fulfilling Prophecy

"Okay…now what?"

*D*ream big. Plan smart. Make it happen. Now that you've had a real chance to explore and consider some of the incredible promotional opportunities that exist within your reach, you are in an excellent position to draw even sharper conclusions about what will work best for you as you grow.

The question is no longer *"Can you do it?"* You *know* you can. And, now that you realize that you have what it takes to find a way or make one, there's really nothing that can stop you—*except you.*

So, get out of your own way!

At this stage of getting there, the issues that can make or break you are nearly the same now as they have been since you first started out, only, of course, they have become a bit more sophisticated. Luckily, your knowledge base and your skill sets have become more refined along the way, too. The truth is, you've never been in a better place to face the important areas you need to consider next. What are the areas to pay attention to now?

- Your attitude
- Your time management
- Your energy level
- Your reaction to change.

Start with your attitude. Remember, even if you are a brain surgeon, PR isn't brain surgery—PR can and should be tremendous fun. If it's not enjoyable, do something about it—stop, back up, and see where you made the wrong turn.

You are meant to do what you're doing for a reason. Sure, the stakes may be higher now, consuming more time, money, and energy than in the past. But, right here and right now, one thing will impact your future happiness forever.

That one thing is your attitude.

Don't let you and your attitude become hopelessly tarnished by the wear and tear of the world. If you are starting to drag, dust off the most important parts of what you're doing—the passion and the fun! Take an objective look at what it means to believe in yourself. Celebrate your potential and recognize your opportunities.

Protect your time. Don't allow unmanaged time to overwhelm and drown you. By now, you've sensed that there's an ebb and flow to what's going on. You've probably dreamed about finding a way to make the tides of motion and time somehow work in your favor. With some effort, it's actually possible to get ahead of the next wave.

Start simply.

Every inch forward is progress made in the right direction. Each bit helps. Begin by taking a look at the calendar for the next year. Mark any and all dates that are meaningful to you. As time goes by, commitments that are marked in advance will help you clearly understand your availability to participate in events as they arise. When you safeguard your time, you are really doing what it takes to protect and nurture your attitude.

Control your energy. Don't allow exhaustion to be the thing that yanks the rug out from under you. The closer you are to where you want to be, the more you must do to conserve your own energy. You need to take proactive steps to reduce the risk of burnout. Ask yourself these four questions:

1. **Are you exhausted for an unreasonable amount of time?** If you aren't sure if an unreasonable amount of time is figured by weeks, months, or years, you have a problem. An unreasonable amount of time is fourteen days straight. Your exhaustion may start as a mental, emotional, or physical response. If you find you know which type visits you most often, which type is your least favorite, and what it's like to have all three kinds of exhaustion simultaneously—well, you've got way too much experience at being exhausted. Learn to say "no," set boundaries, and guard your time.

2. **Are you spending too much time second-guessing yourself?** There may be valid reasons to doubt yourself. But you have a problem when you hear yourself spouting remarks like: "I don't know why I thought I could do this." "I don't know what made me think I had any talent." "I can't believe I am so stupid." Recognize that exhaustion plays a major role whenever you start feeling hammered by feelings of insecurity. Do something to permanently relieve the exhaustion. Get rest, take a new look at your goals, and purposefully celebrate every achievement you've made.

3. **Are you feeling painfully cynical about the present and future?** You may have just realized that "We're all in this together" really means that "We're all in this alone…really alone…especially me." If you are smiling and shaking hands with people that you'd rather kick across the room, and you suspect that everyone else feels the same way, you're in a stage of burnout that requires immediate action. Temporarily remove yourself from the scene. You need to put on the brakes and take a break before you sabotage your own efforts.

4. **Do you feel hopeless and trapped?** Your level of burnout is severe when you have an epiphany in which you clearly understand what they really meant when they said, "I'm damned if I do, and damned if I don't." You need to get some real relief if you find yourself muttering "I give up" or "I'm in too far to ever get out alive" or "My work is very, very important and no one but me can do it." Enough, already. Get the help you need to change the situation or get out of it. This kind of mental and emotional stress is not healthy and it can trigger physical illness. Life's too short to be lived at this level for any length of time. You need to back up—maybe way, way up.

Remember, it's completely natural to experience some tough times. You're bound to find places along the way where you slow down, get stuck, and have to plod along anyway. You don't have to suffer burnout if you take care of yourself, watch your pace, and conserve your energy. By weathering the journey, the process itself is actually preparing you to handle your next level of success.

Manage change proactively. As success becomes more imminent, you need to know that with each new level of success comes a tsunami of emotions associated with getting there.

Mainly, don't forget that you're human—and so are the people around you. Humans have some natural reactions to change, especially dramatic change like the kind that success can bring. Sometimes when you experience change—even the good kind of wonderful change you've always wanted—you may find yourself feeling frantic. Sometimes, when other people see how much you are changing, they may surprise you by acting different. As changes happen, you'll likely experience some universal feelings and you'll encounter some common situations that happen when people become more successful.

Don't be alarmed. Some signs that success is unfolding and that your success is becoming visibly apparent to those around you are when people say things like:

- Well, you must be making a lot of money.
- I guess I can say, "I knew you back when."
- You probably don't care about this little stuff anymore.
- How does it feel to have arrived?
- Will you forget about us now that you're moving in the fast lane?

These remarks may range from sharp to wistful to resentful to cheerful to proud to concerned. Remember that your attitude can make or break you. It's important at every turn to take care of your emotions. When you start hearing these kinds of remarks, it's a good time to express your gratitude for what you've got, how far you've come, and to reflect upon and acknowledge the help you've received along the way.

You can begin to manage change proactively when you realize what to expect. For example, the very moment when things fall perfectly into place usually feels different than you might imagine. Things falling into place often feel like things falling on your head. Who knew? Now you do, so don't get ruffled when it happens.

In fact, get proactive. Find out more about what to expect.

Others have been on the exact same road you're on now, even if they aren't in the same field or facing your specific obstacles. Where do you find these experienced souls? They are in your neighborhood, in your business communities, and all around you.

Connect with them.

You'll find advice and know-how in some funny places. Some of the best is located in fabulous children's books. You'll likely see your own personal tale (and mine) unfold with gentle humor and amazing clarity and style. Try reading *The Carrot Seed* by Ruth Kraus, *The Missing Piece Meets the Big O* by Shel Silverstein, and *Oh, The Places You'll Go* by Dr. Seuss.

Listen to great music. Music helps you to know that you aren't alone—that you are headed in the right direction. You can hear your story sung in a hundred different voices. On my personal journey, some of my most important songs are *Vienna* by Billy Joel, *God Bless the Broken Road* by Rascal Flatts, *I Hope You Dance* by Leann Womack, *Won't Back Down* by Tom Petty, and *World On Fire* by Britt Nicole.

Listen carefully and you, too, will find one or more songs that absolutely resonate with you about where you are and how you feel; it will refresh you to know that you are indeed on a timeless trail traveled by many people who have found their own way.

Just like you.

COACHING CLINIC #18

Here's something you can do right now to navigate your way into the future. The following takes you through the process of identifying your next set of priorities, lining up your focus points, and defining your next round of dreams. Organize your time on a twelve-month calendar.

Consider the following time-related issues:

1. **Personal time.** If you record on your calendar birthdays and other special days that should be reserved, you're less likely to disappoint yourself and your loved ones by making commitments that conflict with these priorities. People you care about come first. In the blur of the moment, next Tuesday may not register as your anniversary, your kid's first day in kindergarten, or your best friend's birthday. Get these things on the calendar *now*.

   What you are really doing here is protecting the feelings of the ones you love. Enter some special reminders on your calendar so that two weeks or so before each of your personal dates, you have time to recognize the coming event with a card or gift or a call. You'll be glad you did. They will, too.

Here are some things to record:

- Birthdays
- Anniversaries
- School-related events
- Work-related events
- Faith-related events
- Personal holiday celebrations and parties.

2. **Business time.** Go over your business calendar and add special references to industry events. Take a look at the seasonal cycle of your industry. Consider trade shows. Note the busy and the slow seasons that are specific to your industry.

3. **Travel time.** Note the places you might reasonably go, when you might go there, why those places interest you, and who you should meet while you're in a certain location. You can ink in the actual arrival and departure details later. The big thing is reserving a block of time that doesn't get filled up with some other activities.

4. **Business development time.** Black out wiggle room to meet production deadlines and schedule time blocks to develop and maintain your contact database every single month. Revisit your notes from Coaching Clinic #17 on building your platform. Consider the growth and the gaps that keep the three legs of your platform from balancing for you. You have to have time to focus on the business development growth you need. Goals won't happen without real effort. You can't make a real effort if the time isn't set aside to allow you to do the work. So set aside the time now:

- Pick three goals that you would like to achieve and assign these goals to dates on which they need to be started or completed, or both.
- Block out eight half-days across the calendar to deliberately attend to moving these chosen goals forward. When you enter the information on the calendar, be precise and detailed enough to be able to recall what you're talking about. Six weeks from now, a quickly scrawled note about today's inspiration may feel confusing and out of sync. It helps when you reference a file or document name so that you can easily find all the information you need to keep your goals moving forward as planned.

Having a series of short, intermediate, and long-term goals help you track progress, stay focused, and move forward.

And that's it!

Now you have the tools and know-how to achieve those dreams that you've thought about for so long. I'm proud of you for believing in yourself. I'm happy that you know that every step counts. The only thing left is to get going—so, go, go, go!

Additional Resources

My Favorite Tools

I love the creativity of the planning process, but I love it even more when tools think like I do, are fun to use, and make the work easier. When managing your own publicity, you've got to share ideas, concepts, and strategic plans with others quickly and simply so you can mobilize yourself and other people. The following is a list of my favorite software. Visit my website (PRTherapy.com) and you can get more information and even download some free trial versions.

SmartDraw

I absolutely love this easy-to-use software. I have used it for years to clearly communicate specific steps in the publicity planning or business development process. I also use it to map out a strategy so a team of people can see roles and goals at a single glance. It's easy to create great-looking business graphics of all kinds in minutes. It truly works just like they claim: Select a template, input your information, and SmartDraw does the rest—aligning everything automatically and applying professional design themes for professional—quality results every time. (SmartDraw.com)

Project KickStart

Brainstorm, plan, and organize your project details. This project management program helps you visualize your promotional process in a different way. So much of your success is tied to having a map—this software helps you create one you can follow. Six planning icons focus your attention on the structure of the project—goals, resources, obstacles, and other strategic issues critical to your project's success. Project Kickstart makes you think about team members, stakeholders, and vendors from the get-go. This program helps you think through the stages of getting to where you want to go. Plus, it's easy to print presentation-ready reports and Gantt charts so you can share your vision with others. (ProjectKickStart.com)

Goal Enforcer

If you feel like you are wearing way too many hats and you may forget something vitally important, sit right down and take a load off your mind. In fact, this software is where you can download the details in your head without allowing anything to get lost. This is the coolest way to recognize, identify, and never lose sight of the step-by-step parts of everything you're trying to do. If you are a visual person, the best thing about this software is that you work with picture objects, instead of lists or columns of information.

Your main goal is represented by a central dark, blue sphere, and all the sub-goals are represented by connected gray spheres. It's easy to set your goals, break down big goals into smaller sub-goals, and track your progress. With a click of the button, the information is converted from spheres to status reports in HTML, XML, comma-separated text, or plain text formats. (GoalEnforcer.com)

Grow Your Business Marketing Plan + Calendar

No marketing plan? No problem. Here's an absolutely excellent downloadable plan and calendar that's ready to use the moment you are ready to begin. Whether you're just starting out, or you have an established business and want to improve your marketing efforts, you need to do outreach year-round—day by day, week by week, month by month, now more than ever. This really cool product offers an appointment calendar that is designed to include solid monthly marketing goals, detailed daily and weekly tasks, and monthly productivity-boosting tips. There are convenient areas to keep track of hot leads and prospects each week, and plenty of space for you to add your unique to-dos. (Marketing-Mentor-Store.com)

Constant Contact

When it's time for an e-mail campaign, Constant Contact makes it easy to look fantastic. Don't have a list of e-mail contacts? Constant Contact can help. They give you the tools you need to start building your e-mail lists immediately and they'll provide you with tools and tips to help you grow your list, too. They have sign-up banners and forms for you to place on your website. Newly collected e-mail addresses are automatically added to your contact list and it's really easy for you to collect additional information, such as birthdays and e-mail list preferences. (ConstantContact.com)

Resources for Speakers

If you're in the early stages of developing your speaking career, or if you want to maximize a travel opportunity to reach people while you are in a particular area, think about connecting in advance with libraries, schools, and nonprofits to arrange a special event. Your destination's local media is more likely to tell their community about you if you are doing something in the area for free or helping raise funds for a hometown charity.

Here are some great resources to help you build your outreach plans:

• **Find Libraries**

At PublicLibraries.com, you'll find a state-by-state directory for public libraries, including a listing for presidential libraries, national libraries of the world, and even links to university and college libraries.

• **Find Schools**

Nces.ed.gov will help you find venues where you can speak to groups of students, parents, or educators. You can search by state, city, and zip code. A special search allows you to sort private schools by religious affiliation, number of students, and grade levels. The College Navigator allows you to narrow choices by institution type, level of degree awarded, private or public, urban or rural setting, religious affiliation, athletic programming, and specialized mission.

• **Find a local Chamber Of Commerce**

Visit ChamberofCommerce.com. Then go to the Resource Directory page and type in the city and state for contact information, membership information, and website links.

• **Find a local Rotary Club**

Go to Rotary.org. The Rotary International is the world's first service club organization. Its more than 1.2 million members volunteer their time and talent to further the Rotary motto: Service Above Self. The club locator page provides contact information for clubs in specific areas. You can also find local Rotary Club website addresses here.

• **Find a local Boys and Girls Club**

Check out bgca.org. Boys and Girls Clubs are truly "The Positive Place for Kids"—and a great place for you to connect with people in the community who care. You can search by zip code for contact information and website links to local clubs.

• **Find a local YMCA**

Visit YMCA.net. The YMCA offers a fun, wholesome forum to get to know the community. You can locate a specific YMCA by zip code for contact information and website links.

• **Look for local nonprofits in any area**

MelissaDATA.com is a great resource to find nonprofits. You can search for nonprofits that serve people with the same demographics as your target market. From the home page, choose "Lookups," and scroll down to find the Nonprofit Organizations link, then enter the zip code for listings by name, IRS subsection, assets, and income. It will help you find venues you never knew existed.

Book Festivals Where You Can Use PR

For writers and other PR seekers who share a target market of people who love to read, book festivals are really fun places, with lots of special networking opportunities. My all-time-favorite book event is the Los Angeles Times Festival of Books, where I've had the pleasure to meet John Wooden, Catherine Coulter, Ray Bradbury, Emeril Lagasse, and dozens of authors of all genres.

If you are an author or qualify as a book-festival speaker or performer, approach the event coordinators about ten months in advance of the event. Don't forget to ask about promotional opportunities that could include a booth or table or inclusion in a printed program. Don't forget to connect with local bookstore vendors who might like to host your special appearance in their booth.

Check these out!
1. Ann Arbor Book Festival (MI)— aabookfestival.org
2. Arizona Book Festival— azbookfestival.org
3. Arkansas Literary Festival— arkansasliteraryfestival.org
4. Baltimore Book Festival (MD)— baltimorebookfestival.com
5. Baltimore CityLit Festival (MD)— citylitproject.org
6. Book Island Festival (FL)— bookisland.org
7. Border Book Festival (NM)— borderbookfestival.org
8. Buckeye Book Fair (OH)— buckeyebookfair.com
9. Celebration of Books (OK)— poetsandwriters.okstate.edu/celebration/index.html
10. Central Coast Book & Author Festival (CA)— ccbookfestival.org
11. Chicago Tribune Printers Row Book Fair (IL)— chicagotribune.com/about/custom/events/printersrow
12. Fall for the Book (VA)— fallforthebook.org
13. Fay B. Kaigler Children's Book Festival (MS)— usm.edu/bookfest
14. Great Salt Lake Book Festival (UT)— utahhumanities.org/BookFestival.htm
15. Indianapolis Book Fest (IN)— indianapolisbookfest.com
16. Kentucky Book Fair— kybookfair.org
17. Latino Book & Family Festival (various locations)— lbff.us
18. Lee County Reading Festival (FL)— www3.leegov.com/library/ReadingFestivalHome.htm
19. Los Angeles Times Festival of Books— latimes.com/extras/festivalofbooks
20. Louisiana Book Festival— lbf.state.lib.la.us
21. Miami Book Fair International (FL)— miamibookfair.com
22. Montana Festival of the Book— humanitiesmontana.org/BookFestival/bookfest.shtml
23. Multicultural Children's Book Festival (DC)— kennedy-center.org/programs/specialevents/bookfestival
24. National Book Festival (DC)— loc.gov/bookfest

25. Nebraska Book Festival— unl.edu/NCB/current_festival.html
26. North Carolina Festival of the Book— ncbook.org/ncbookfestival.html
27. Ohio River Festival of Books— (WV) ohioriverbooks.org
28. Portland Wordstock (OR)— wordstockfestival.com/#/page_id=110
29. Rochester Children's Book Festival (NY)— rochesterchildrensbookfestival.org
30. South Carolina Book Festival— scbookfestival.org
31. Southern Festival of Books (TN)— humanitiestennessee.org/festival
32. Southern Kentucky Book Fest— sokybookfest.org
33. St. Louis Storytelling Festival (MO)— umsl.edu/divisions/conted/storyfes
34. St. Petersburg Times Festival of Reading (FL)— festivalofreading.com
35. Tennessee Williams/New Orleans Literary Festival— tennesseewilliams.net
36. Texas Book Festival— texasbookfestival.org/index.php
37. Twin Cities Book Festival (MN)— raintaxi.com/bookfest
38. Vegas Valley Book Festival (NV)— artslasvegas.org/vvbf
39. Virginia Festival of the Book— vabook.org/index.html
40. West Hollywood Book Fair (CA)— westhollywoodbookfair.org
41. West Virginia Book Festival— wvhumanities.org/bookfest/bookfest2.htm
42. Wisconsin Book Festival— wisconsinbookfestival.org

Websites for Writers

• **WritersMarket.com**—Whether you're looking for publishers to pitch story ideas to or you are writing your own material in hopes of publication, this low-cost service and easy-to-use dashboard provides terrific lists of magazines, newspapers, book publishers, literary agents, and more.

• **WoodenHorsePub.com**—For less than a latte, you can access this gold mine of information that's always kept up-to-date. See editorial calendars and contact information for magazines that are big, small, consumer, trade, national, and regional.

• **MediaBistro.com**—This is an ultra-cool resource of media news—including hints and help for your publicity pitches, a ton of daily newsletters, and a library of mastheads of magazines.

• **MarcelaLandres.com**—Immerse yourself in the latest Latino/Hispanic literary events, contests, and writing opportunities offered by this former Simon & Schuster editor and the author of the e-book *How Editors Think*.

• **CreativeByline.com**— This matchmaking service for writers is a revolutionary way for writers to get their work in front of publishers. The process of manuscript submission is totally streamlined, fun, and inexpensive.

• **Blurb.com**—Download easy-to-use software and create your own bookstore-quality books that are professional, polished, and with production prices that are incredibly affordable. This site affords a memorable way to create a portfolio that showcases who you are and what you do.

• **Writing.com**—Sign up for a free online portfolio, numerous user tools, e-mail services, and a chance to network.

How to Contact Celebrities

Looking for star power? If you think your products or services would be loved by a celebrity, make sure he or she knows about it. If you have a special charitable cause or altruistic mission that you think is shared by a movie star, musician, or renowned public figure, speak up. The first step is finding out how to reach them.

ContactAnyCelebrity.com—This exclusive online database contains the United States Postal Service-verified mailing addresses, agents, managers, publicists, production companies, and favorite charitable causes for nearly 55,000 celebrities and public figures worldwide. It also features weekly Celebrity Gift Bag opportunities, so you can easily get your product into celebrities' hands.

They publish *The Celebrity Black Book*, an annual print directory the contains the mailing addresses for the same celebrities and public figures. Although the online database contains more information and is updated every day, the book is a great resource for those of you who would rather have a real book you can hold in your hands.

Celebrity Leverage Toolkit—This includes sixteen audio CDs and *The Celebrity Leverage Manual*. It will help you get your products and services in celebrities' hands for endorsements, instant credibility, and star-powered publicity. It also reveals how to harness the power of celebrity to make your business—and even yourself—famous. (CelebrityEndorsements.com)

INDEX

ACKNOWLEDGMENTS

The part that is seldom explained about the joy of following your passion and dreams is that much of the journey will feel like you're strapped onboard Mr. Toad's Wild Ride. That's why it is so important to surround yourself with exceptional people who are also funny and fun. I've been lucky enough to do what I love…with people who are extraordinary.

Special thanks to my favorite people:
Our kids Alex, Chelsea, Garrett (and, of course, Sparky).

My mom Onnie and the entire family.

All my buddies, friends, and clients,
especially those who chose to join me on Mr. Toad's Wild Ride
for particularly enjoyable spins, memorable seasons, or an entire wild lifetime:
Susan Johnston Mixson; Rebecca Forster; Jen Singer;
Richard Tyler Jordan; Melanie Geiss; Suzanne Helmig; Cheryl Bradley;
Gladys Doherty; Shannon Martin; Herb, Jr. and his legendary dad Herb Nero;
Marcela Landres; Chris Edwards; Hazel Dixon Cooper; Karen Rauch Carter;
Marybeth Hicks; Vicki Medina; Nick Owchar; Rich Edler; Cindy Himmelberg;
Craig Harris; Marjorie K. Diamond; Tim Engle Frank Dixon; Dennis
Anderson; Bill Wu; Jay Duke; Bill Warford; Jenni Moran; Arlyn Imberman;
Jamie Novak; Franklin Silverstone and the Collectify gang; Dr. Jennifer
Holtzman; Shane Idleman; Sylvia Mendoza; Irwin Zucker; Kelly and Laura
Freas; Lynn, Randy, and Donald Tivens; Sharon Surber, Frank Campbell, Julie
Still, and Mila. The Entire ReDiscover Gang, especially Alan Flory and Bev
Hatley Linda Pollock, Linda Lego, Jason Ward, and Debby Tangblade. And,
certainly, the wonderful Holiday Homes crew.

And, of course, agent, business partner, and good friend, June Clark, who has
passionately launched and cultivated many lifetimes of dreams, including so
many of mine. And, finally, Kent Sorsky and Steve Mettee, and the entire
wonderful team at Quill Driver Books.

ABOUT THE AUTHOR

For more than a decade, Robin Blakely has provided promotional services for best-selling authors, award-winning screenwriters, renowned artists, CEOs from multimillion-dollar companies, scholars, and creative talents from across the country. President of Livingston Communications, Inc. and a founding partner of New York City-based Get There Media, Robin has secured and managed placements for clients at print, broadcast, and live venues, including HGTV, the *Los Angeles Times* Festival of Books, the National Baseball Hall of Fame, the *Hollywood Reporter*, ABC World News, *Vanity Fair*, Book TV, and more. The focus of Robin's consulting practice is to help individuals build authentic relationships with their target audiences through traditional and new media.

Visit her at **PRTherapy.com**